The Expo.

EPHESIANS

Life In The Heights

Dr. Glen Spencer Jr.

SPENCER'S EVANGELISTIC MINISTRIES

15 Pine Ridge Road – Tunkhannock, Pa. 18657

Phone:. (570) 333-4263 –EMAIL: GraceForLiving@epix.net

Ephesians: Life In The Heights
Copyright © 2011 by Glen Spencer Jr.

All Scripture Quotations From The King James Bible

Contents

Recommendations From Our Readers

Pastor Spencer is not only a gifted preacher, but a gifted writer as well. As a fundamentalist and pastor, I am careful about the books I endorse, but Dr. Spencer is at the top of my list of writers. So, it is with great honor that I recommend his Expository Pulpit Series to you.

Michael D. McClary, Th.D,
Pastor, Community-Bainbridge Baptist Church,
Founder/Executive Director, Good Samaritan Ministries

I have enjoyed reading your books in the past and look forward to getting newer ones. The thing I enjoyed about your books were that when I read them I said, "I have to teach this to my people. I want others to know this". I appreciate your study, work and insight.

Dr. Jeff Fugate
Pastor, Clays Mill Road Baptist Church
President of Commonwealth Baptist College

Dr. Glen Spencer's Bible commentaries are valuable for today. They are expository, edifying and exciting in aiding the Christian, the teacher and the preacher to understand the mind of God and to become victorious in their daily lives. I will use the complete set.

Dr. Bruce Miller, Evangelist
President of Atlantic Coast Baptist College

It is with great delight that I recommend to you, "The Expository Pulpit Commentary Series." Dr. Glen Spencer Jr. combines years of exhaustive research and practical ministry experience to bring to the church, the pastor, the teacher, and the student of the Scriptures a sound, in-depth and yet very practical set of study tools. This ongoing verse by commentary series will be a great addition to your library. This is not just more rehashed information but wise insight from a seasoned Bible Scholar. I know Dr. Glen Spencer Jr. the man and have found him to be a great Christian, a compassionate pastor and a true champion of the authorized King James Bible, believing it to be God's Preserved Word For English speaking people.

This trustworthy commentary series is, Dispensational in theology, pre-Tribulation and pre-millennial in its eschatology, literal in its hermeneutical approach and expository in its format. I am thrilled that this good work is now available to you and I as we seek to benefit from its invaluable help to deepen our knowledge of God's perfect, preserved word.

Dr. Jon M. Jenkins,
Pastor, Grace Baptist Church
President of Grace Baptist College

"You have written an excellent study on the Book of Revelation. This will be a great help to preachers and teachers everywhere. This work is informative, inspiring, and encouraging. Your alliterative outlines are excellent! Your study of this book will be a great help to many, many Christians."

Dr. Lee Roberson
Founder of Tennessee Temple University

The Salutation
Ephesians 1:1-2

Paul begins the epistle to the Ephesians with the call and will of God for his life.

THE APOSTLE

Paul, an apostle of Jesus Christ... (Ephesians 1:1a) The word **apostle** means *"sent one."* In the New Testament the word primarily refers to one who had a direct commission from Christ as did Paul (Acts 26:16-18). In stressing his apostleship, Paul was affirming his call and claiming the Lord's authority for his preaching. Besides the original twelve and Matthias (Acts 1:26), who replaced Judas, Paul was the only other apostle. He said, **Am I not an apostle? am I not free? have I not seen Jesus Christ our Lord? are not ye my work in the Lord? (1 Corinthians 9:1)** Contrary to the teaching of some, there are no apostles today.

THE ASSURANCE

Paul's life and actions were in accordance with ...**the will of God. (Ephesians 1:1b)** Paul had absolute assurance that he was in God's will. Every child of God needs to know and do the will of God. Christ is our example in being surrendered to the will of God. Even though it meant terrible pain, suffering and separation from God He said, ... **Father, if thou be willing, remove this cup from me: nevertheless not my will, but thine, be done. (Luke 22:42)** The priority of Christ's life was to obey the perfect will of God. Jesus was able to say, ... **for I do always those things that please him. (John 8:29)** What a testimony we would have if we would simply set our hearts to love and do the will of God. When we walk as Christ walked in obedience to the Word and will of God we please Him.

THE ADDRESSEES

This letter is addressed ... **to the saints which are at Ephesus, and to the faithful in Christ Jesus: (Ephesians 1:1c).** Ephesus was the capitol of the Roman province of Asia Minor. Because it was a major port city, it was a place of tourist trade. There was a constant flurry of activity as the crowds would come and go. Not only was Ephesus a major commercial hub, but she was the religious center of the Roman world. The temple of the fertility goddess Diana was there and the city was filled with the filthy practices of their hedonist religion.

This letter to the **saints ... and to the faithful in Christ Jesus.** This is refreshing in light of the wickedness of the city. In spite of the fact that Ephesus was a satanic stronghold, there were faithful believers there. **Saint** is a common New Testament designation for Christians. The word **saint** comes from the same word as separation and holy. All of these words have the same root meaning of *"being set apart."* The furniture of the Tabernacle was said to be holy. That is, it was separated from any common use and set apart for the service of God. The word saint has nothing to do with what we personally have merited or accomplished. It is all God's doing. The moment we are saved, God sets us apart from the world and unto Himself.

THE ACKNOWLEDGEMENT

Grace be to you, and peace, from God our Father, and from the Lord Jesus Christ. (Ephesians 1:2) This is a familiar salutation in many of the New Testament epistles. (Romans 1:7, 1 Corinthians 1:3, 2 Corinthians1:2, Galatians 1:3, Philippians 1:2; Colossians 1:2) **Grace** and **peace** are two of the sweetest words in the English language—grace and peace. **Grace** is simply the unmerited favor of God. G. Campbell Morgan said, *"Grace is the river flowing from the heart of God."* Grace is God doing for man that which he cannot do for himself. Where would we be without grace?

Then there is **peace.** Paul knew real peace and the origin of it. Paul could wish them peace but he could not give them peace. That must come from **God our Father, and from the Lord Jesus Christ.** It is only after one has by God's grace been forgiven of his sins and made a new creature in Christ that he can experience true peace. **Therefore being justified by faith, we have peace with God through our Lord Jesus Christ: By whom also we have access by faith into this grace wherein we stand, and rejoice in hope of the glory of God. (Romans 5:1-2)** The world knows nothing of this kind of peace and joy. Where God has not worked and divine grace transformed the heart there is no real peace. **There is no peace, saith the LORD, unto the wicked. (Isaiah 48:22)**

To the believer Jesus said, **These things I have spoken unto you, that in me ye might have peace. In the world ye shall have tribulation: but be of good cheer; I have overcome the world. (John 16:33)** Paul's peace came from an unwavering trust in the Saviour who has overcome the world. True and lasting peace is the fruit of a right relationship with God.

We've Got Something To Shout About
Ephesians 1:3

This next section of 12 verses is filled with precious truths concerning the believer's riches in Christ. In the Greek New Testament these twelve verses comprise one long and unbroken sentence. Paul lists the benefits and blessings of being a child of God. This one sentence of 264 words overflows and floods our soul with the truth of God's goodness. Leon Tucker said:

> "... much like the book itself, scaling heights and spanning breadths unknown! ... The study of it will reveal great grammatical construction. One truth will, in this sentence give birth to another, all bound together in philosophical precision and by the laws of powerful association. This sentence is as a wheel within a wheel; complete yet always coming to completion. The sentence is built upon a series of participles, each participle adding another link to the chain, until, as it were, all is forged. The scope of the sentence is from one eternity to another! It reaches from before the foundation of the world to the consummation of the ages. There is the elaboration of every great truth of revelation in this one sentence. What depth of revelation awaits our meditation! "

Looking at verse 3 we notice five truths.

THE SHOUT

Blessed be the God and Father of our Lord Jesus Christ... (Ephesians 1:3a) This is a joyous ascription of praise to God.

This is a celebration of praise to God for His goodness and blessings upon an unworthy people. This is a shout of worship and adoration. It is the shout of a praise filled heart exploding to the glory of God. It is only natural that such praise flow from the heart of the redeemed. We live in a time when many Churches are spiritually dead. There is not a lot of excitement about the things of God. Many mistake emotionalism for praise. We must understand that emotionalism and praise are two different things. True praise will involve the emotions, but an emotional fit is not true praise. Praise and worship is something that comes from the heart. In essence true worship is an outward expression of an inward affection. Until the heart is not only full, but flooded with love and praise for God there will be no real manifestation of true worship. Plain and simply put worship is a matter of the heart. David said, **I was glad when they said unto me, Let us go into the house of the LORD. (Psalm 122:1)** This is the norm of the Christian life—to be glad and excited about the things of God.

> **Enter into his gates with thanksgiving, and into his courts with praise: be thankful unto him, and bless his name.. (Psalm 100:4)**

> **Praise ye the LORD. Praise God in his sanctuary: praise him in the firmament of his power. (Psalm 150:1)**

> **Praise him for his mighty acts: praise him according to his excellent greatness. (Psalm 150:2)**

> **Praise him with the sound of the trumpet: praise him with the psaltery and harp. (Psalm 150:3)**

> **Let every thing that hath breath praise the LORD... (Psalm 150:6)**

Imagine Paul as he sits in his prison cell at Rome contemplating the things of God when all at once he breaks out in praise and worship. He wasn't in a fancy church building. He didn't have a worship leader. He wasn't on an emotional high. There was no rock band present. It was just him and God. God flooded Paul's heart and he broke forth in a crescendo of praise that few could understand. True worship comes from praise-filled hearts of the redeemed.

THE SOURCE

The source of our blessings is **the God and Father of our Lord Jesus Christ, who hath blessed us. (Ephesians 1:3b)** Anything that is good comes from God. **Every good gift and every perfect gift is from above, and cometh down from the Father of lights, with whom is no variableness, neither shadow of turning. (James 1:17)** My friend, this is the God of Heaven we are talking about here. We can take this to the bank. Leon Tucker tells of an old Scotch saint, when asked if she did not presume upon God when she insisted upon the assurance of her salvation said, "My salvation was an eternal arrangement between God the Father and His Son and they who counseled it and commenced it will continue and conclude it." If you are saved you are as sure of Heaven and glorification as if you were already there.

THE SUBJECTS

Who are the recipients of His blessings? It is **...us. (Ephesians 1:3c)** Those who have been saved by the wonderful grace of God can lay claim upon these many blessings. How do we even put into words the goodness of God towards His people? In view of the vastness of creation and the surpassing glory of God as Creator David asked,

What is man, that thou art mindful of him? and the son of man, that thou visitest him? (Psalm 8:4) This is a rhetorical question emphasizing the insignificance of man, but God's compassion, concern and care for him nevertheless. **LORD, what is man, that thou takest knowledge of him! or the son of man, that thou makest account of him! (Psalm 144:3)** In another place David said, **... every man at his best state is altogether vanity. Selah. (Psalm 39:5)** The Psalmist marveled at the thought that the Holy God of Glory would even take note of us, let alone help us.

THE SUPPLY

As God's children we are the recipients of **all spiritual blessings. (Ephesians 1:3d)** Not some spiritual blessings, but **all.** As a child of God we lack nothing that God intends for us to have. The moment we were saved, He gave us everything. Talk about being rich—the believer was born rich. It's tragic that many believers live as though they are bankrupt beggars instead of a child of the King. In the Guinness Book of World Records, a woman by the name of Hetty Green is listed as the world's greatest miser. She died in 1916, leaving an estate worth over one hundred million dollars. Although extremely rich, she argued over every bill she received and finally her own lawyers had to sue her to collect their legal fees. On her 21st birthday she refused to light the candles on her birthday cake so as not to waste them. The next day she wiped the cake off the candles and returned them to the store for a refund. When her son Ned was 14, he sustained a leg injury in a sledding accident. Hetty refused to take him to a hospital and instead tried to treat the injury at home and finally by taking him to a free clinic. As a result, his leg had to be amputated. When she died they found a small tin in her bathroom filled with slivers of soap she saved to compress together to avoid buying a new bar of soap. She is said to have once spent half a night looking for a two-cent stamp that she had misplaced. What a sad life of misery and want! To possess such great wealth, but live like a pauper.

Yet, how many Christians, though rich in heavenly assets live like spiritual paupers. Dead, dull, dry, and deprived describes a lot of Christians and it need not be. Imagine walking around a billionaire and either not knowing it or being unwilling to access your account. This is such a problem that Paul prayed for the Ephesian believers along these lines. **The eyes of your understanding being enlightened; that ye may know what is the hope of his calling, and what the riches of the glory of his inheritance in the saints. (Ephesians 1:18)** My friend you may not have much by way of material things, but when you were born again, you were born rich.

THE SPHERE

We are blessed with all spiritual blessings **in heavenly places. (Ephesians 1:3d)** The expression **in heavenly places** occurs four times in the book of Ephesians (1:3, 20; 3:10; 6:12), but nowhere else in the entire New Testament and speaks of the invisible realm. In the context it speaks of the third Heaven where God resides. H. G. C. Moule said, *"The form of the adjective suggests not only a heavenly origin, but a heavenly locality."* Our riches are safe in Heaven. This particular text speaks of the vast storehouse of riches that are ours in Christ. Jesus went beyond our inherited riches and spoke of our adding to it. **But lay up for yourselves**

treasures in heaven, where neither moth nor rust doth corrupt, and where thieves do not break through nor steal. (Matthew 6:20) Either way, notice that our inheritance and our rewards are safe in Heaven.

THE STANDING

We note that all blessings are found **in Christ. (Ephesians 1:3e)** Oliver B. Greene points out that:

> "The statement 'in Christ Jesus' (or the same statement expressed in other words) appears fourteen times in the first chapter of Ephesians. 'In Christ Jesus' is the key that unlocks this storehouse of spiritual blessings. In Christ Jesus is the key that opens the door and permits us to look into the storehouse of this Epistle."

This phrase refers to our standing (our position) in Christ. We are **in Christ.** What blessed words these are! Though our locality is here on earth our actual position is in Christ in the heavenlies. This is our spiritual position. There are no spiritual blessings outside of Christ! Because we are in Christ we have all that He has. God help us to live this life as though we are heavenly people.

My Father Planed It All
Ephesians 1:4-6

Here Paul states that our election and adoption were planned by God before the foundation of the word.

HE APPOINTED US

Here is a subject that stirs up a great deal of passion and discussion.

God's Plan In Choosing Us

The word **chosen** has the sovereignty of God written all over it. We must not miss the point of this verse. It does not mean that God chose to save some while letting the rest go to Hell. Imagine a God who says that He will save **whosoever will** and then turn around and select some, while arbitrarily foreordaining the rest to Hell without a chance. Such is not the God of the Bible. God is presented as a loving Saviour, Who is ... **not willing that any should perish, but that all should come to repentance. (2 Peter 3:9)** The word **chosen** simply speaks of the fact that God made a sovereign choice to save the lost. Notice that God ... **hath chosen us in him before the foundation of the world. (Ephesians 1:4b)** God's choice to save man took place before the world was ever created. We must consider the basis for God's choosing.

> **Elect according to the foreknowledge of God the Father, through sanctification of the Spirit, unto obedience and sprinkling of the blood of Jesus Christ ... (1 Peter 1:2)**

> **For whom he did foreknow, he also did predestinate to be conformed to the image of his**

Son, that he might be the firstborn among many brethren. (Romans 8:29)

It is the doctrine of God's **foreknowledge** that clears up the inconsistencies of man's teaching. The foreknowledge of God is the basis for His election. Based upon anything except God's foreknowledge, predestination would be fatalistic, depriving man of his free will choice.

In eternity past God looked down the hallway of time and saw you and me. He saw that we were dead in trespasses and sin and condemned to die. He planned to send His only begotten Son to this earth to die in our place. God saw us in eternity. He saw us one day presented with the choice of receiving Jesus Christ. He heard some say no to Christ and heard others say yes. Those whom He foreknew would say yes, God chose in Christ to be saved and conformed to Christ. This is where God's sovereignty and man's free will is reconciled. **Known unto God are all his works from the beginning of the world. (Acts 15:18)** Notice the Holy Spirit inspired order of foreknowledge and predestination.

Elect according to the foreknowledge... (1 Peter 1:2)

For whom he did foreknow, he also did predestinate... (Romans 8:29)

There are those who flip these verses around to suit their theology. They attempt to teach that God foreknew the elect because He had pre-selected them to be saved. However, we see that foreknowledge comes first. It does not say, *"Foreknowledge according to His election,"* nor does it say, *"Whom He did predestinate them also He did foreknow."* It is clear that God's election and choosing and predestination are all based upon His foreknowledge. God looked down through the ages and He saw who would be saved and He saw who would not. Before the foundation of the world He foreknew who would trust Christ. It is those whom God foreknew that He elected. When one divorces election from foreknowledge he ends up with fatalism.

God's Purpose In Choosing Us

Paul says, **...that we should be holy and without blame before him in love. (Ephesians 1:4c)** Holiness is the aim of God for His people. He did not save us to remain what we were. We have imputed righteousness that God applies to our account when we exercise faith in Christ (2 Corinthians 5:21). But there is also practical righteousness that we must work at obtaining.

> **That ye put off concerning the former conversation the old man, which is corrupt according to the deceitful lusts; And be renewed in the spirit of your mind; And that ye put on the new man, which after God is created in righteousness and true holiness. (Ephesians 4:22-24)**

> **But put ye on the Lord Jesus Christ, and make not provision for the flesh, to fulfil the lusts thereof. (Romans 13:14)**

We are to put off the works of the flesh and put on the Lord Jesus Christ. We are to replace the bad with the good. We are challenged to walk according to what we are rather than what we were.

HE ADOPTED US

Having predestinated us unto the adoption of children by Jesus Christ to himself, according to the good pleasure of his will. (Ephesians 1:5) Here we have the word predestined, but notice that we are predestined to **adoption.** Salvation and adoption are two completely different works.

1) **Salvation** means *"to deliver; to salvage."* It is the act of God whereby He salvages man from the bondage of sin and the penalty of eternal damnation.

2) **Adoption** is the act of God, whereby He receives us into His family and bestows upon us all the rights and privileges of sonship.

Adoption has to do with our position. We are born of God and every believer is a child of God. John said, **But as many as received him, to them gave he power to become the sons of God, even to them that believe on his name. (John 1:12)** Praise God! When we are saved we become Children of God. Paul said to the Romans, **For ye have not received the spirit of bondage again to fear; but ye have received the Spirit of adoption, whereby we cry, Abba, Father. (Romans 8:15)** Adoption indicates a family relationship. In Paul's day adoption was a judicial act whereby a father would publicly bestow upon his son the full privileges and responsibilities as a member of the family.

HE ACCEPTED US

To the praise of the glory of his grace, wherein he hath made us accepted in the beloved. (Ephesians 1:6) Once again we find God's grace to be the motivating factor behind His actions. The **beloved** is Jesus Christ. When God accepted us it was on the merit of Christ's redemptive work. **To the praise of the glory of his grace** stresses the fact of His goodness and mercy. We could not make ourselves accepted in the beloved—God had to do it. Grace is God doing for man that which he cannot do for himself.

Redeemed By The Blood
Ephesians 1:7-13

The Blood of Jesus Christ is one of the great subjects of Scripture. It is one of the fundamentals of our faith. The liberals and modernists discount and deny the blood atonement. They tell us that the shedding of Christ's blood was nothing more than a symbol of His death. However, the Bible is clear when it comes to sin that **without shedding of blood is no remission. (Hebrews 9:22)** Without the shed blood of Jesus Christ, there is no salvation.

THE REDEMPTION

In whom we have redemption through his blood, the forgiveness of sins. (Ephesians 1:7a) The whole human race is a family of bankrupt beggars. All that God intended us to be, Adam lost to the devil in the Garden of Eden. We were left naked, poor, and miserably lost in sin. We could in no way or by no means pay the price for our salvation. Left to himself, man is helpless and hopeless, lost and sentenced to spend eternity in a devil's hell. The Bible declares that, ... **the Son of man came not to be ministered unto, but to minister, and to give his life a ransom for many. (Matthew 20:28)** There on the cross Jesus fulfilled the one great purpose of His coming—giving Himself and shedding His blood as a ransom for sinners. How clearly He stated the purpose of His coming. **I am the good shepherd: the good shepherd giveth his life for the sheep...and I lay down my life for the sheep. (John 10:1 & ,15)** Christ gave Himself in death as the great ransom for the world, which was under the curse of sin and subject to eternal death and damnation, but God stepped in. Just think of where we would be without God. **But God, who is rich in mercy, for his great love wherewith he loved us, Even when we were dead in sins, hath quickened us together with Christ, (by grace ye are saved;) (Ephesians 2:4-5)** Let's take note of a few points concerning redemption.

The Possession

As believers salvation is a possession that **we have** right now. Once we are saved salvation becomes a sure thing. We are not just hoping everything works out and we get to Heaven someday. Under inspiration of the Holy Spirit John wrote, **These things have I written unto you that believe on the name of the Son of God; that ye may know that ye have eternal life, and that ye may believe on the name of the Son of God. (1 John 5:13)** Praise God! The Bible teaches a **KNOW SO** salvation. What a tragedy that so many are without Bible assurance concerning their salvation. The Bible teaches that we can know for sure whether or not we are saved. Along with salvation there is personal assurance. John said, **Beloved, now are we the sons of God. (1 John 3:2)** There is a lot of assurance wrapped up in this statement. If you are saved you are (present tense) His child **NOW.** Take notice, John does not say, We shall be sons of God. He does not say, We hope to be the sons of God. Oh no! He presents the truth that, **Now are we the sons of God.** The very moment that the sinner turns to Christ as his Saviour, he is born again into the family of God. At that moment and forever he is a child of God. **But as many as received Him, to them gave He power to become the sons**

of God, even to them that believe on His name. (John 1:12) Sonship is a present possession.

The Purchase

The word **redemption** speaks volumes. It is a word that speaks of paying the ransom to release a slave from bondage. In order to set a slave free a satisfactory payment has to be made. The sinner himself cannot make a satisfactory payment for his sin. The curse of the law rests heavy upon us all—we are or were under the bondage of sin. **Cursed is every one that continueth not in all things which are written in the book of the law to do them. (Galatians 3:10)** Oh! How impossible is for sinful and fallen man to obey the law of God. The curse was upon us all for **all have sinned and come short of the glory of God. (Romans 3:23)** The debt of sin must be paid and we being sinners cannot pay the price. The best that we can do, God cannot accept (Isaiah 64:6).

The Payment

Our salvation is secured **through his blood.** God could not accept our works as an atonement for sin, but He could accept as a satisfactory payment the atonement of the Sinless One—Jesus Christ. The blood of Christ met and satisfied the justice and holiness of God. Speaking of Christ the Bible says, **And he is the propitiation for our sins: and not for ours only, but also for the sins of the whole world. (1 John 2:2)** The word **propitiation** carries the idea of satisfaction. Relating to salvation God's righteous demands had to be satisfied and we see here that it is Christ who met that demand of sinless perfection and satisfied God. Noah Webster defines **propitiation** as: *"The act of appeasing* *wrath and conciliating the favor of an offended person; the act of making propitious."*

Paul spoke of our propitiation in his letter to the Romans. **Being justified freely by his grace through the redemption that is in Christ Jesus: Whom God hath set forth to be a propitiation through faith in his blood, to declare his righteousness for the remission of sins that are past, through the forbearance of God. (Romans 3:24-25)** Here Paul says we are, **justified freely by his grace through the redemption that is in Christ Jesus.** To redeem means to pay a satisfactory price for a person or thing. Jesus Christ purchased redemption for man by paying the price demanded and satisfying the demands of the law. The law demanded the death penalty, and Jesus Christ, God's sacrificial Lamb, took the sinner's place and paid that penalty in full. Therefore we are justified freely by His grace through the redemption which is in Jesus Christ.

The Pardon

The result is **the forgiveness of sins. Forgiveness** is one of the most precious words in the Bible. In our context it is closely related to the word redemption. Forgiveness means *"to release from bondage or imprisonment."* It carries the idea of releasing and sending away. The illustration of God sending our sins away was seen in the Old Testament. Back in Israel on the Day of Atonement, the high priest took two goats. First the priest killed one of the two goats and sprinkled it's blood before God on the mercy seat. Then he placed his hands on the other goat's head, confessing the people's sins and then sent the goat into the wilderness never to be seen again. (Leviticus 16:1-27) The scapegoat representing man's sin was forever gone, never to return.

That is what God did when He forgave our sins—He sent them away never to return. **As far as the east is from the west, so far hath he removed our transgressions from us. (Psalm 103:12)**

The forgiveness of our sins upon trusting Christ is a guarantee of God. The Bible states that, **If we confess our sins, he is faithful and just to forgive us our sins, and to cleanse us from all unrighteousness. (1 John 1:9)** If a Christian will take God at His Word and confesses his sins, God will cleanse him of **all unrighteousness.** Notice the big word **ALL**. In His grace and mercy God includes all sin in His forgiveness—not some unrighteousness, but **ALL** unrighteousness. Forgiveness and cleansing are guaranteed to anyone for any sin. This is based upon God's faithfulness to keep His promises. The cleansing spoken of here is that which comes from the shed Blood of Christ. **But if we walk in the light, as he is in the light, we have fellowship one with another, and the blood of Jesus Christ his Son cleanseth us from all sin (1 John 1:7)**

THE RICHES

Everything that the believer has is **... according to the riches of his grace. (Ephesians 1:7b)** Focus for a moment on that phrase **according to riches of His grace.** What an immeasurable thought! Lehman Strauss said, *"No adequate explanation of divine forgiveness can be made apart from those beautiful and precious words."* Redemption and forgiveness of sins are **according to the riches of his grace.** Notice it is not from His riches but **according to** the riches of His grace. Bill Gates is one of the richest men in the world with a net worth of over fifty billion dollars. If Bill Gates were to contribute to a worthy cause, and he gave a check for

$200.00, he would only be giving from his riches. But if, instead, he gave a check for $200,000.00, he would be giving according to his riches. Charles Hodge spoke of this abundance as *"an overflowing abundance of unmerited love, inexhaustible in God and freely accessible through Christ."*

God never gives from, but according to His riches. God's grace is as boundless as He is. **Where sin abounded, grace did much more abound. (Romans 5:20)** . The word abound carries the idea of *"super abounding"* and means to *"surpass by far, exceed immeasurably,* or *overflow beyond."* God is infinitely rich and the extent of His forgiveness is determined by the **riches of his grace.** There is no sin that His grace cannot surpass and no need that He is unable to satisfy. Because God is infinite, His grace is infinite.

THE REASONING

Wherein he hath abounded toward us in all wisdom and prudence. (Ephesians 1:8) As a result of salvation we can have a deeper understanding and reasoning concerning the things of God. Everyone, even unbelievers have some reasoning power. God commanded unbelievers to:

> **Come now, and let us reason together, saith the LORD... (Isaiah 1:18)**

However, to understand the deep things of God man must have the discernment that comes from the indwelling Holy Spirit. Paul said to the Corinthians:

> **Which things also we speak, not in the words which man's wisdom teacheth, but which the Holy Ghost teacheth; comparing spiritual things with spiritual. But the natural man receiveth not the things of the Spirit of God: for they are foolishness**

unto him: neither can he know them, because they are spiritually discerned. But he that is spiritual judgeth all things, yet he himself is judged of no man. (1 Corinthians 2:13-15)

Spiritual discernment is the great need of the hour. Paul gives several facts concerning wisdom and discernment.

Acquiring Of Wisdom

The word **wisdom** according to Liddell and Scott, carries the idea of *"skill in matters of common life."* J. Armitage Robinson defined wisdom as *"the knowledge which sees into the heart of things, which knows them as they really are."* The general idea is that of a workman having ability and skill at what he does. In Biblical context, wisdom is the God given ability to use knowledge properly.

Application Of Wisdom

The word **prudence** speaks of *"practical discernment."* Wisdom and prudence are closely related, but different. **I wisdom dwell with prudence, and find out knowledge of witty inventions. (Proverbs 8:12) Noah** Webster defines **prudence** as:

> "Wisdom applied to practice. Prudence implies caution in deliberating and consulting on the most suitable means to accomplish valuable purposes ... Prudence differs from wisdom in this, that prudence implies more caution and reserve than wisdom, or is exercised more in foreseeing and avoiding evil, than in devising and executing that which is good."

Prudence is the practical discernment and insight that enables us to avoid evil. **A prudent man foreseeth the evil,** and hideth himself: but the simple pass on, and are punished. (Proverbs 22:3)** Both, wisdom and prudence come from learning and knowing the Word of God. Jesus said, **Ye do err, not knowing the scriptures... (Matthew 22:29)** The Apostle Paul said under inspiration of the Holy Spirit, **So then faith cometh by hearing, and hearing by the word of God. (Romans 10:17)** It is through the Word of God that the believer is taught and corrected. **Now ye are clean through the word which I have spoken unto you. (John 15:3)** The only way to be fruitful in our Christian walk is to live a life based upon God's Word.

THE REVELATION

Having made known unto us the mystery of his will, according to his good pleasure which he hath purposed in himself: That in the dispensation of the fulness of times he might gather together in one all things in Christ, both which are in heaven, and which are on earth; even in him. (Ephesians 1:9-10) Notice the wording **having already made known.** The action described in verse nine took place before the action of verse eight. In other words, He made known unto us the mystery of His will, then He abounded toward us with wisdom and prudence. Upon our receiving Christ and being saved God begins to reveal His will to us, the **mystery of His will.** A **mystery** is something that was previously hidden, but now revealed. Many of the truths and blessings we have in the Church Age were unknown in the Old Testament. God knew of the Church and all the great truths associated with it, but so far as the world was concerned, it was a mystery—it was unknown. But now He has made it known unto us. The secret things of God are hidden from those who are outside the family of God.

That in the dispensation of the fulness of times he might gather together in one all things in Christ, both which are in heaven, and which are on earth; even in him. (Ephesians 1:10) This speaks of a time (**in the dispensation of the fulness of times**) when Christ will gather the totality of all creation into unity. Right now it is divided and lost—sin has marred the wonderful creation of God. But the time is coming when God will **gather together in one all things in Christ.** This includes the earth, the animals, man, and solar systems. **For the earnest expectation of the creature waiteth for the manifestation of the sons of God. For the creature was made subject to vanity, not willingly, but by reason of him who hath subjected the same in hope, Because the creature itself also shall be delivered from the bondage of corruption into the glorious liberty of the children of God. For we know that the whole creation groaneth and travaileth in pain together until now. (Romans 8:19-22)** All things will be made new by Jesus Christ Himself. **And he that sat upon the throne said, Behold, I make all things new. And he said unto me, Write: for these words are true and faithful. (Revelation 21:5)** All creation will be delivered from the curse of sin and set free. The unbeliever has a hard time comprehending this truth, the redeemed, however, can understand and even desire the consummation of the ages.

THE RESULTS

In whom also we have obtained an inheritance, being predestinated according to the purpose of him who worketh all things after the counsel of his own will: (Ephesians 1:11) We have been adopted into the family of God and are His children. Therefore we have an inheritance.

In Christ we have everything that He has. In fact the Bible describes the child of God as **... joint-heirs with Christ. (Romans 8:17)** Peter speaks of our inheritance as, **... an inheritance incorruptible, and undefiled, and that fadeth not away, reserved in heaven for you. (1 Peter 1:4)** As joint-heirs, everything that God has given to Christ He has given to us. **He that spared not his own Son, but delivered him up for us all, how shall he not with him also freely give us all things? (Romans 8:32)**

THE REJOICING

That we should be to the praise of his glory, who first trusted in Christ. (Ephesians 1:12) All that God has done for us should result in **the praise of his glory.** That is what Paul is doing in these 13 verses. He is praising God and giving Him the glory for all that God has done. This is whole-hearted praise. David said, **I will praise thee, O LORD, with my whole heart; I will shew forth all thy marvellous works. (Psalms 9:1)** If God's people would be as vocal about God as they are about their favorite ball team, God would get the glory He deserves. **Give unto the LORD the glory due unto his name; worship the LORD in the beauty of holiness. (Psalm 29:2)**

Sealed By the Holy Spirit
Ephesians 1:13-14

In our text, the Holy Spirit is likened to a seal. In the ancient world a seal guaranteed authenticity. Many kings wore a signet ring with his royal seal engraved on it. Once the king's signature was given, the document was sealed by pressing the signet ring into the soft wax on the document. Sealing was used to authenticate contracts, for new laws, military orders and anything of importance requiring the King's signature. The seal was also used in the ratification of treaties. Immediately upon trusting Jesus Christ as Saviour the new Christian is sealed with the Holy Spirit. As applied to the Christian there are three great truths concerning the seal of the Spirit.

THE SEAL SPEAKS OF POSSESSION

Once the believer is placed into Christ, the Holy Spirit seals him permanently. Therefore, the seal of the Holy Spirit is God's mark of ownership. This seal signifies that the believer has been bought by the precious blood. The Bible declares, **ye are not your own? For ye are bought with a price. (1 Corinthians 6:19b-20a)** We often hear people say, "*It is my body and I will do with it as I please.*" When you purchase something it belongs to you. Jesus Christ purchased our salvation and we belong to Him. **Ye are not your own** is an established fact. The Bible says, **Ye are bought with a price.** There was a great price paid that sinners might be redeemed from the slave market of sin. Peter reminds us of the price paid:

> **Forasmuch as ye know that ye were not redeemed with corruptible things, as silver and gold, from your vain conversation received by tradition from your fathers; But with the precious blood of Christ, as of a lamb without blemish and without spot. (1 Peter 1:18-19)**

What Jesus Christ did for us in the shedding of His blood is, for the most part, beyond our comprehension. We can explain it to a degree by using terms such as love, grace and mercy. However, we still fall far short of fully understanding God's love. We know it is real, we know it works and we know what it has done for us, but who can sufficiently put it into words. What a great God we have! **The LORD hath appeared of old unto me, saying, Yea, I have loved thee with an everlasting love: therefore with lovingkindness have I drawn thee. (Jeremiah 31:3)** When the day came for the sins of man to be paid for, it was God who paid the redemptive price with the blood of Christ. Not one sin has ever been forgiven apart from the blood of Christ. No wonder Peter calls the blood of Christ **precious.** Remember what God says about it, **...ye are not your own? For ye are bought with a price. (1 Corinthians 6:19b-20a)**

The ownership indicated by a seal is seen in the words of Christ, **I am the good shepherd, and know my sheep, and am known of mine. (John 10:14)** The Lord knows His own. **Nevertheless the foundation of God standeth sure, having this seal, The Lord knoweth them that are his... (2 Timothy 2:19)** Just as cattle are sometimes given a brand as a seal of ownership, the believer is given the Holy Spirit as a seal of

God's ownership. **But ye are not in the flesh, but in the Spirit, if so be that the Spirit of God dwell in you. Now if any man have not the Spirit of Christ, he is none of his. (Romans 8:9)**

THE SEAL SPEAKS OF A PLEDGE

The Holy Spirit is the **earnest of our inheritance.** The word **earnest** speaks of a pledge or a guarantee. The word is a legal and commercial term that refers to a down payment made as a pledge of full payment. It is the guarantee of the purchaser's promise and intent to follow through on the entire transaction. The meaning of this sealing is shown in the Old Testament. Upon a king sealing a document it became an official legal transaction (1 Kings 21:8), and it was unalterable. **Now, O king, establish the decree, and sign the writing, that it be not changed, according to the law of the Medes and Persians, which altereth not. (Daniel 6:8)** Once the king's signature was given, the document was sealed by pressing the signet ring into the soft wax on the document. The seal was proof of the authenticity of the document and was legally binding. So when the Spirit seals the new child of God, his standing in Christ is unalterable. The presence of the Spirit in the believer is God's pledge that he will receive a full inheritance.

THE SEAL SPEAKS OF PERMANENCE

The seal speaks of a finished transaction. This is absolute security. **And grieve not the holy Spirit of God, whereby ye are sealed unto the day of redemption. (Ephesians 4:30)** Sealed for how long? The text says, **unto the day of redemption.** The **day of redemption** speaks of the finalization of salvation when even the body is redeemed.

The soul is redeemed now, but the body will not be redeemed and delivered until the rapture. **And not only they, but ourselves also, which have the firstfruits of the Spirit, even we ourselves groan within ourselves, waiting for the adoption, to wit, the redemption of our body. (Romans 8:23)** The body is not redeemed yet. However, the seal of the Spirit guarantees our full and complete redemption. Once the King put his seal on something it could not be changed. Even the King himself could not change it (see Daniel 6:14-17). **Being confident of this very thing, that he which hath begun a good work in you will perform it until the day of Jesus Christ. (Philippians 1:6)** The believer's salvation is an eternal gift.

A Good Testimony
Ephesians 1:15

Paul starts out by saying, **I heard.** What a testimony! Paul was continuing to hear good reports about the Ephesian Church. In these reports two great qualities stood out.

THEY EXERCISED FAITH IN CHRIST

Paul said, **I heard of your faith in the Lord Jesus ... (Ephesians 1:15a)** The common characteristic that bonds believers together is their faith in the Lord Jesus Christ. Believers are united together in Christ by faith. There is an initial faith that one exercises in the Saviour when he is first saved. However, the faith Paul specks of here is probably their continuing faithfulness to Christ. Their faith was evident in their faithfulness. That is what James meant when he said, **... I will shew thee my faith by my works. (James 2:18)** This is what God expects from the believer—to be faithful. **Moreover it is required in stewards, that a man be found faithful. (1 Corinthians 4:2)** A steward is a person who has been entrusted with the management of another's affairs and possessions. The manager oversees and reports to the owner and is a steward of that business. Our Lord has entrusted us with wealth and resources to promote the cause of Christ. Faithfulness involves serving Him in a way that He gets a return on His investment. Faithful is something every believer is supposed to be. Faithfulness means *"being steadfast in your affection or allegiance, being loyal to a cause or a person—being constant, loyal and* *persistent—trustworthy."* Applied to the believer it means being the kind of Christian God can trust!

THEY EXHIBITED LOVE FOR ONE ANOTHER

Not only did their faith stand out, but also their ... **love unto all the saints. (Ephesians 1:15b)** Love is one the main qualities that proves we are God's people. True Biblical love is evidence of the new birth. **Whosoever shall confess that Jesus is the Son of God, God dwelleth in him, and he in God. And we have known and believed the love that God hath to us. God is love; and he that dwelleth in love dwelleth in God, and God in him. (1 John 4:15-16)** J. W. Kanoy said, *"God's wonderful love does not end with Calvary. It flourishes and is perfected within us."* John said, **For this is the message that ye heard from the beginning, that we should love one another. (1 John 3:11)** This is Biblical love, not the world's love and not even ecumenical love, but Biblical love. **Be kindly affectioned one to another with brotherly love; in honour preferring one another. (Romans 12:10)** I heard a little poem that pretty much sums up the way many Christians feel about the matter of loving the brethren today.

To dwell above with saints we love,

That will be grace and glory.

To live below with saints we know;

That's another story!

Some folks are hard to love—they make it hard to love them. However, Biblical love is a characteristic of the Christian. On the night of the Lord's Supper, Jesus revealed to the disciples that He would soon die. He then instructed them, **A new commandment I give unto you, that ye love one another; as I have loved you, that ye also love one another. By this shall all men know that ye are my disciples, if ye have love one to another. (John 13:34-35)** Notice that our Lord calls this a **new** commandment. The command to love one another was not new. So far as man is concerned love is as old as the law. Moses said, **... thou shalt love thy neighbour as thyself. (Leviticus 19:18)** The command to love was new because Jesus gave it a new standard. Grace always carries a greater responsibility than law. No longer do we love each other as we love ourselves, but Jesus said to **love one another; as I have loved you.** He loved us all the way to the cross. His is a sacrificial love. **Greater love hath no man than this, that a man lay down his life for his friends. (John 15:13)** It is one thing to say I love you, but it is quite another to show it. God not only said I love you; He demonstrated His love for us. **But God commendeth his love toward us, in that, while we were yet sinners, Christ died for us. (Romans 5:8)** Jesus left us with the responsibility to love one another the same way. Jesus also said, **By this shall all men know that ye are my disciples, if ye have love one to another.** In our love for one another the world should see God's love for them. Our love for each other is evidence that we are His disciples. As Oliver B. Greene wrote:

> "The person who does not have a heart of love need not pretend that he is a believer, for God is love and if a man knows God, then God abides in his heart; and the person with God in his heart will love in deed and in truth, not just in word. When God abides in the

heart, love automatically issues from the heart. Never has so much meaning, so much truth, been crowded into three short words: God is love."

Bear in mind that the word translated love is agape. Its essence is to love the object whether or not it is lovable. That is the way God loved us. (John 3:16; Romans 5:8) Many people are not lovable, but it is our duty to love them anyway, just as Christ does. God has enabled us to love the unlovely. Because of salvation, those who have never loved can now love because the love of God is shed abroad in our hearts by the Holy Ghost which is given unto us. (Romans 5:5) On the other hand, a professing Christian who hates his brother is not saved. Instead he is considered a murderer by God and **no murderer hath eternal life abiding in him.**

Some Things We Need
Ephesians 1:16-23

Paul had a fervent prayer life and prayed fervently for the Ephesian Church. He said, I **Cease not to give thanks for you, making mention of you in my prayers; (Ephesians 1:16)** Paul had just told them about their tremendous and bountiful blessings in Christ. Now, he prays that they would fully know and appreciate those blessings. In this prayer we see some things we need.

ENLIGHTENED WITH THE PLAN OF GOD

The Biblical illiteracy of our day is a sad thing. Even among those who profess to be Christians, there is an overwhelming ignorance concerning truth. Paul's prayer was that such ignorance would not be the case among the Ephesians. Paul prayed that, **The eyes of your understanding being enlightened. (Ephesians 1:18a)** The word **enlightened** means *"illuminated; instructed; enlightened; informed; furnished with clear views."* To be enlightened with the plan of God involves three areas.

Requires God's Wisdom

That the God of our Lord Jesus Christ, the Father of glory, may give unto you the spirit of wisdom and revelation in the knowledge of him: (Ephesians 1:17) There are three words used here in connection with enlightenment.

First, the ***Application Of Wisdom***. **Wisdom** is the ability to apply knowledge. It is the God-given ability to practice what we know to be truth. We must not mistake knowledge for wisdom! Wisdom enables us to understand and to discern what to do, how to do it, and when to do it. Wisdom is essential for living the Christian life. James said, **If any of you lack wisdom, let him ask of God, that giveth to all men liberally, and upbraideth not; and it shall be given him. (James 1:5)**

Second, the ***Abundance Of Revelation***. The word **revelation** means *"to uncover, expose, disclose, or make known."* It carries the idea of removing a veil and exposing that which is hidden behind it. Revelation is God revealing to man what he would otherwise never know. God has taken the cover off and revealed the great truths that mankind needs to know. God has given us His Inspired, Infallible and Inerrant word. The revelation of God is complete. There are no new revelations today. **But when that which is perfect is come, then that which is in part shall be done away. (1 Corinthians 13:10)** The Word of God is His complete revelation to man.

Third, the ***Acquiring Of Knowledge***. **Knowledge** is the information we need to live for God. God has given us His Word, now we must dig into it and learn it. We are commanded to, **Study to show thyself approved unto God, a workman that needeth not to be ashamed, rightly dividing the word of truth. (2 Timothy 2:15)** A Christian who stays in the Word of God is referred to as a **workman that needeth not to be ashamed.** On the other hand it is a shameful thing to have the Word of God and neglect the study of it. Jesus said, **Ye do err, not knowing the scriptures... (Matthew 22:29)** God help us to be students of His Word.

Wisdom, Revelation and **Knowledge** are available, but we must go to the right source. Christ taught us that the Spirit of God and the wisdom of God go together. (John 14:26; John 16:12-15) To be enlightened with the plan of God we must be filled with the Spirit of God and draw from the Word of God.

Results In God's Will

Paul says, **that ye may know what is the hope of his calling. (Ephesians 1:18b)** Our enlightenment will result in a greater understanding of the calling of God in our life. Every believer has **hope** and **calling**. Keep in mind that the word **hope** in the Bible does not mean *"hope so,"* like a child hoping for a doll or a bike at Christmas. The word carries with it *"assurance."* The word **calling** has the idea of a "vocation or a work." Every Christian has a purpose and place in the work of God. However, many Christians miss their calling because they do not know the will of God.

Reveals God's Wealth

Paul prayed that they might understand **... the riches of the glory of his inheritance in the saints. (Ephesians 1:18c)** What riches we have in Christ! All of our needs are supplied **... according to his riches in glory by Christ Jesus. (Philippians 4:19)** God's riches are inexhaustible and there is not one need we could ever have that He cannot supply. That is what we have now, but we also have an **inheritance** reserved in Heaven for us. As we are enlightened with the plan of God, our focus is drawn away from the here and now and our hearts are fixed on the there and then. Though we may not have large bank accounts and we may not have everything we want, we do have as Peter said, **an inheritance incorruptible, and undefiled, and that fadeth** not away, reserved in heaven for you. (1 Peter 1:4) God wants us to be enlightened as to the wealth and glory of our coming inheritance.

EQUIPPED WITH THE POWER OF GOD

And what is the exceeding greatness of his power to us-ward who believe, according to the working of his mighty power, Which he wrought in Christ, when he raised him from the dead, and set him at his own right hand in the heavenly places. (Ephesians 1:19-20) Think about this! The same power of God that resurrected Christ from the dead and exalted Him to His throne is available **to us-ward who believe.**

The Capacity

And what is the exceeding greatness of his power... (Ephesians 1:19a) There are no limits to God's power so far as God is concerned. Paul speaks of God's power in terms of **exceeding greatness.** The word **exceeding** means *"going beyond; surpassing; excelling; outdoing ... great in extent, quantity or duration; very extensive."* It is sad that the average Christian knows very little if anything about the reality of God's power. There are three words used in verse 19 to describe the power of God.

1) The word translated **power** is the word from which our English word *dynamite* is derived. It is used here to describe the omnipotent all-powerfulness of God.

2) The word **working** speaks of the operational power of God—what God's power accomplishes.

3) The word **mighty** speaks of *"ability, might, power, strength."*

Old fashioned Holy Ghost power is the need of the day. The Bible frequently refers to God's power as it relates to the believer.

> **But ye shall receive power, after that the Holy Ghost is come upon you: and ye shall be witnesses unto me both in Jerusalem, and in all Judaea, and in Samaria, and unto the uttermost part of the earth. (Acts 1:8)**

> **Finally, my brethren, be strong in the Lord, and in the power of his might. (Ephesians 6:10)**

> **Whereunto I also labour, striving according to his working, which worketh in me mightily. (Colossians 1:29)**

God intends that His work be accomplished by His power. We live in a day when denominations, Churches, and religious organizations are running on man-made programs, social agendas, and orders handed down from denominational headquarters. The average ministry is fueled by the flesh. The Word of God is scarcely preached while rock music and religious performers entertain worldly pagans. Such activity is a far cry from what God intended and expects the local Church to be. No amount of worldly noise or manmade programming will make up for the sad lack of the Holy Spirit's presence. Samuel Chadwick writes:

"The Church that is man-managed instead of God-governed is doomed to failure. A ministry that is College-trained but not Spirit-filled works no miracles. The Church that multiplies committees and neglects prayer may be fussy, noisy, entertaining and enterprising, but it labours in vain and spends its strength for naught. It is possible to excel in mechanics and fail in dynamic. There is a superabundance of machinery; what is wanting is power. To run an organization needs no God. Man can supply the energy, enterprise and enthusiasm for things human. The real work of a Church depends upon the power of the Spirit."

There are too many Christians trying to do the work of God without first being filled with God. If we are to ever see revival we must have the power of God. The power of God in our lives is the result of being Spirit filled and we are commanded to be filled with the Spirit. **And be not drunk with wine, wherein is excess; but be filled with the Spirit. (Ephesians 5:18)** The filling of the Holy Spirit will result in power for service with souls being won to Christ and Christians growing in grace and knowledge. No one can do the work of God successfully without being filled with the Holy Spirit.

The Channel

The power of God is **to us-ward. (Ephesians 1:19b)** Do we fully understand this? The Divine power of God is channeled to **us** who are the children of God. This means that I have to my advantage the same power of God that resurrected Christ from the dead and exalted Him to His throne.

First, I can ___Walk For Christ___. The Bible says, **Walk in the Spirit, and ye shall not fulfil the lust of the flesh. (Galatians 5:16)** Here we see the sharp contrast between the Spirit and the flesh—the two natures in the believer. When God saves us He does not destroy the old depraved nature which we receive at our natural birth. God does, however, impart to the new believer an absolutely new nature, born of the Holy Spirit of God. The old nature was not altered or changed at salvation, neither can it be reformed. The Bible tells us that the only method for dealing with the old nature is crucifixion. Paul said, **I am crucified with Christ: nevertheless I live; yet not I, but Christ liveth in me: and the life which I now live in the flesh I live by the faith of the Son of God, who loved me, and gave himself for me. (Galatians 2:20)** Again, to the Romans, Paul wrote, **For if ye live after the flesh, ye shall die: but if ye through the Spirit do mortify the deeds of the body, ye shall live. (Romans 8:13)** The old nature must be put off. It can be crucified and controlled, but it cannot be reformed.

The believer can, however, overcome the flesh and live a Spirit-filled life. Jesus said, **That which is born of the Spirit is spirit. (John 3:6)** This is the new birth when one becomes a **partaker of the divine nature. (2 Peter 1:4)** The new nature cannot and will not sin because it is born of God. **Whosoever is born of God doth not commit sin; for his seed remaineth in him: and he cannot sin, because he is born of God. (1 John 3:9)** When the believer sins it is because he submits and succumbs to the old nature. However, when we walk in the Spirit we have victory and overcome the flesh. **Walk in the Spirit, and ye shall not fulfil the lust of the flesh. (Galatians 5:16)** Every temptation, every trial, every terror can be met with the Divine power of God.

Second, I can *Work For Christ*. **But ye shall receive power, after that the Holy Ghost is come upon you: and ye shall be witnesses unto me both in Jerusalem, and in all Judaea, and in Samaria, and unto the uttermost part of the earth. (Acts 1:8)** The Holy Spirit works through the believer to win others to Christ. The Bible states that the Holy Spirit **will reprove the world of sin, and of righteousness, and of**

judgment. (John 16:8) As God's people we must get a hold on this truth. Where the Holy Spirit is not at work to convict the lost of their sinful condition and need of salvation there will be no souls saved. It is only as the believer surrenders to and is filled with the Holy Spirit to overflowing that He can flow out and into the lives of others. **In the last day, that great day of the feast, Jesus stood and cried, saying, If any man thirst, let him come unto me, and drink. He that believeth on me, as the scripture hath said, out of his belly shall flow rivers of living water. But this spake he of the Spirit, which they that believe on him should receive: for the Holy Ghost was not yet given; because that Jesus was not yet glorified. (John 7:37-39)** As long as we grieve, quench and suppress Him in our lives there will be no real fruit. It is only as we give Him full control of our lives that He can flow through us to others.

The Condition

The power of God is to those **... who believe. (Ephesians 1:19c)** This is a condition for the victorious life. In referring to those **who believe** Paul goes beyond the initial act of faith in God for salvation and speaks of a continuing and growing faith. There are a good number of folks who have believed and been saved who's faith hasn't grown. Right here is where the average Christian fails. The faith that saves is not the faith whereby we live the victorious Christian life. Our faith must grow.

Everyone has faith, though little it may be. The Bible teaches that God has put within the heart of every man a measure of faith. **For I say, through the grace given unto me, to every man that is among you, not to think of himself more highly than he ought to think; but to think**

soberly, according as God hath dealt to every man the measure of faith. (Romans 12:3) Everyone is born into this world with a measure of faith. This does away with the foolish notion that only an elect and elite group can be saved. God, Who desires that all men be saved, (2 Peter 3:9) has given to everyone the faith whereby they may of their own free will choose to accept the free offer of salvation. It is by that measure of faith that one accepts the finished work of Christ as the atonement for his sin. **For by grace are ye saved through faith….. (Ephesians 2:8a)** At the very moment one exercises faith in Christ he is born again and becomes a Christian. However, the work of faith does not stop there, this is where it starts. Saving faith must grow into something bigger. Faith must be exercised in all areas of Christian growth. Saving faith is sufficient for trusting Christ and being saved, but such must grow into **Sanctifying faith**, **Serving faith**, **Standing faith**, and **Suffering faith**. It takes far more faith to encounter and endure the battles of the Christian life than it did to trust Christ and be born again. Why is there such a power shortage among professing Christians today? Why is there so little power when God states that He has given us His Divine power? Too many people are trusting Christ for the power to save their souls and not trusting Him for the power to live day by day.

The power of God is most neglected resource in the Church. Leon Tucker wrote the following words back in 1917:

> "Power is the one thing the church of God needs most and has least. The work of the Lord languishes for lack of power. The church, like Samson in the lap of a harlot, has divulged the secret of strength and is shorn of power. The church cannot arise and go out

as at other times, and this the Philistines well know."

Do you have the power of God in your life? If not, why not? It is available. **...Walk in the Spirit, and ye shall not fulfil the lust of the flesh. (Galatians 5:16)** Obeying that command would settle the matter of walking in the flesh verses walking in the Spirit. The text is clear! If we do walk in the Spirit we will not **fulfil the lust of the flesh.** Herein lies the means of victory! **WALK IN THE SPIRIT.** The next thing we need is to be ...

ENAMORED WITH THE PERSON OF GOD

Paul wanted them to know more than the power of Christ, he also wanted them to know the person of Christ.

Our Lord's Prominence

Speaking of Christ, the Bible says that God **... set him at his own right hand in the heavenly places, Far above all principality, and power, and might, and dominion, and every name that is named, not only in this world, but also in that which is to come. (Ephesians 1:20b)** This speaks of Christ's exaltation—He is superior to all. Specifically, here, Christ is superior to all **principality, power, might,** and **dominion.** These were traditional Jewish terms referring to supreme powers—including the powers of the Satan's kingdom and the demon world. This is an important passage for the believer who desires to have victory in the Christian life. Just like Christ is physically seated at the right hand of God in Heaven, the believer is spiritually seated there.

> **But God, who is rich in mercy, for his great love**
> **wherewith he loved us, Even when we were dead**
> **in sins, hath quickened us together with Christ,**

(by grace ye are saved;) And hath raised us up together, and made us sit together in heavenly places in Christ Jesus. (Ephesians 2:4-6)

So certain is the believer's arrival in Heaven that God already sees us there. We are even now seated in the place of victory with Christ. Since Christ's power and authority far surpasses the satanic forces that seek to destroy the child of God, Christians can have full assurance of ultimate victory.

Our Lord's Position

And hath put all things under his feet... This speaks of Christ's Lordship. Tragically, the Lordship of Christ is the most neglected and forsaken doctrine of our day. Those who waste so much time debating Biblical Lordship and repentance will quickly lose their argument when they stand before Christ. **Wherefore God also hath highly exalted him, and given him a name which is above every name: That at the name of Jesus every knee should bow, of things in heaven, and things in earth, and things under the earth; And that every tongue should confess that Jesus Christ is Lord, to the glory of God the Father. (Philippians 2:9-11)** Lordship and repentance are hard doctrines for the world to accept because they require submission and change. Any doctrine that runs against the grain of man's depravity will be a discarded and detested doctrine. However, one cannot honestly study the Bible without coming to the conclusion that Jesus Christ is Lord. Lordship requires submission and repentance requires change. Lordship says, Jesus is Lord— submit to Him. Repentance says, stop doing what you are doing and start doing right. To claim the benefits of salvation without an obedient and changed life makes one guilty of lying and hypocrisy. **And why call ye me, Lord, Lord, and do not the things which I say? (Luke 6:46)**

Our Lord's Preeminence

God gave Christ **to be the head over all things to the church, Which is his body, the fulness of him that filleth all in all.** This speaks of Christ's headship. Christ is the Head of the Church. Christ's being the Head of the Church is a parallel to the physical body. (1 Corinthians 12) The head determines what the body will do and works through the body to accomplish it's will. Here God says, **the fulness of him that filleth all in all.** The word **filleth** carries the idea of *"accomplishing, completing, or bringing something about."* Notice that this action of *"accomplishing, completing, or bringing something about"* is the responsibility of God's people. The context is clear! Just like the physical head accomplishes it's will trough the physical body, during the Church age, Christ, as the head of the Church, accomplishes His will through the Church. He has purposely limited Himself to what He can accomplish through His people. Are you obedient or are you a crippled member of the body of Christ?

Our Wonderful Salvation
Ephesians 2:1-10

In chapter one Paul told us what we have in Christ. He spoke of the great truths of Adoption, Redemption, our Inheritance, etc. In chapte   r two, Paul starts by reminding us of our condition before salvation and continues on to establish the fact that salvation is by grace alone.

THE CONDITION OF THE SINNER

The phrases **and you (2:1)**, and **but God (2:4)** paint for us one of the most precious and satisfying pictures in the Word of God. We can never completely appreciate who we are in Christ until we fully comprehend what we were without Him. The first three verses describe the natural man in his depraved and lost state. Our pre-conversion condition was not a pretty one.

We were Dead

And you hath he quickened, who were dead in trespasses and sins; (Ephesians 2:1) In the Word of God, there are three kinds of death:

1) **Spiritual death**—the separation of the spirit from God (Ephesians 2:1, 4:18; 1 John 5:12)

2) **Physical death**—the separation of the soul, or life, from the body (1 Corinthians 15:21-22; Hebrews 9:27)

3) **Eternal death**—the eternal separation of the soul from the presence of God (Revelation 20:14,15; 2 Thessalonians 1:9)

The sinner is **dead in trespasses and sins.** The sinner is spiritually dead—his sin has separated him from God. Some take this verse to extremes and teach what they call the total inability of man. Their contention is that a dead man is dead and therefore has no ability to make a choice. For certain, the Bible clearly teaches that a lost man is incapable of saving himself. However, he can still exercise his freewill in choosing to accept or reject Christ as Saviour. (Isaiah 1:18)

The Bible clearly teaches that the believer is also dead to sin. **God forbid. How shall we, that are dead to sin, live any longer therein? (Romans 6:2)** This is fact! The Child of God is dead to sin. Does that mean that the believer does not sin? Absolutely not! Being dead to sin does not mean that he is totally unable to sin. The fact is the believer in Christ often chooses to sin. To be **dead to sin** does not mean that a believer is totally unable to sin, it means that Christ has separated him from the slavery of sin and set him apart for a specific purpose.

To be dead in trespass and sins simply means that the lost are separated from God by their sin. **But your iniquities have separated between you and your God, and your sins have hid his face from you, that he will not hear. (Isaiah 59:2)** The very minute Adam partook of the fruit of the tree of the knowledge of good and evil he died. Death was the penalty of his choice. **But of the tree of the knowledge of good and evil, thou shalt not eat of it: for in the day that**

thou eatest thereof thou shalt surely die. (Genesis 2:17) He experienced death in his spirit immediately, he experienced death in his soul gradually, and he experienced death in his body inevitably. He was dead, but he was still breathing, he was still walking around, he was still making choices. In fact, he was conscience of the fact that he had done wrong and knew that he would have to answer to God for it. He even tried to cover himself with the works of his own hands when he made the fig leaf aprons. However, he had a major problem—his sin had separated him from God. He was now a sinner **dead in trespasses and sins** and there was nothing that he could do about it. However, when God made for Adam and Eve **coats of skins, and clothed them,** they accepted the covering and were saved.

We were Deceived

Wherein in time past ye walked according to the course of this world... (Ephesians 2:2a) The word **walked** speaks of lifestyle—our way of life before salvation. Our way of living was characterized by sin. The word **world** is not speaking of the planet, but the world system and its standards. Paul uses the same idea in Galatians referring to **this present evil world. (Galatians 1:4)** He is referring to the evil system that is under the leadership and control of Satan. It is that which is completely opposed to God. This is how we walked before salvation. It was our lifestyle. We didn't know any better—we were deceived. A little later Paul wrote, **This I say therefore, and testify in the Lord, that ye henceforth walk not as other Gentiles walk, in the vanity of their mind, Having the understanding darkened, being alienated from the life of God through the ignorance that**

is in them, because of the blindness of their heart. **(Ephesians 4:17-18)** Salvation cleans us up and life takes on a whole new direction and meaning.

We were Dominated

Before salvation we walked **...according to the prince of the power of the air. (Ephesians 2:2b)** This world talks a lot about freedom, but knows little about it. Those who claim to be free from God are worst captives of all—they are captives of Satan. A lot of folks are in error concerning the existence and personality of Satan. Many laugh and jeer at the idea of a personal Devil. They refer to him as a figment of the imagination, an influence, or as I heard one poor soul say, "just another teaching of the Fundamentalists." My friend, it was not a figment of the imagination that tempted Eve to eat of the forbidden tree. Nor was it a figment of the imagination that the Lord Jesus Christ contended with in the wilderness.

Many do not even believe in Satan, yet he is their god. **But if our gospel be hid, it is hid to them that are lost: In whom the god of this world hath blinded the minds of them which believe not, lest the light of the glorious gospel of Christ, who is the image of God, should shine unto them. (2 Corinthians 4:3-4)** Satan dominates the unsaved world. He is the god of this present evil system—the system that every unsaved person is subject to.

We were Disobedient

As a result of Satan's dominance the lost are driven by ... **the spirit that now worketh in the children of disobedience: Among whom also we all had our conversation in times past in the lusts of our flesh,**

fulfilling the desires of the flesh and of the mind; and were by nature the children of wrath, even as others.. (Ephesians 2:2c-3) The natural man has no ability to live for God. Even when he wants to do right he is incapable of doing so because he does not have the Spirit of God. Even if unsaved man wants to be good and do right, he is powerless to do so. It is not until we come to Christ and receive the enabling of His Spirit that we can overcome.

Unfortunately believers can also be disobedient and unbelieving. This is why Paul warned us in Ephesians 4:17-19, that our manner of life must not parallel that of the unbelievers. Disobedience results in broken fellowship with God and weakens us to the place that we, even as Christians can be dominated by Satan. Such was the case with Peter when Jesus said to him, **… Get thee behind me, Satan: thou art an offence unto me: for thou savourest not the things that be of God, but those that be of men. (Matthew 16:23)** Peter was a child of God, but he was dominated by Satan, even to the point that Jesus addressed Satan through Peter.

THE COMPASSION OF THE SAVIOUR

Immediately after describing the depravity of man and his fallen condition, the inspired writer says, **But God.** What a contrast! Robert L. Deffinbaugh said, *"the words, 'But God' … are a beacon of light and hope in a sea of despair."* Right in the midst of sinful misery God steps on the scene.

An Undeserved Mercy

The first thing we see is that our God is **rich in mercy. (Ephesians 2:4a)** Dr. Lehman Strauss defines mercy as, *"God's exercise of pity and compassion upon the sinner with* *a forbearance he does not deserve."* God so loves and pities lost sinners that He withholds His judgment and extends His gracious invitation to be saved. Indeed He is the **Father of mercies. (2 Corinthians 1:3)**

Not only is He a God of mercy, but He is **rich in mercy,** not just having a good measure of mercy, but having excessive wealth in His mercy. The word **rich** comes from *"plooseeos"* and carries the idea of *"abounding with."* God abounds with mercy. Moses said, **The LORD is longsuffering, and of great mercy, forgiving iniquity and transgression... (Numbers 14:18)** Peter wrote, **Blessed be the God and Father of our Lord Jesus Christ, which according to his abundant mercy hath begotten us again unto a lively hope by the resurrection of Jesus Christ from the dead. (1 Peter 1:3)** The idea is that of an inexhaustible supply. It is an overflowing mercy that extends far beyond our sin. See Psalm 103:8-18 where God's mercy is described.

An Unselfish Love

We are reminded of God's **great love wherewith he loved us. (Ephesians 2:4b)** Our sin is black, filthy, and repulsive, yet our souls are precious to Him. This is a selfless and sacrificial love, a love which gives itself for the object of its love. **For God so loved the world, that he gave his only begotten Son, that whosoever believeth in him should not perish, but have everlasting life. (John 3:16)** God's love has not merely been proclaimed, but demonstrated. How was it demonstrated? He gave us His Son. **But God commendeth his love toward us, in that, while we were yet sinners, Christ died for us. (Romans 5:8)** God put principle into picture when He offered Jesus Christ as a substitute for our sin. Love is the very essence of God. God doesn't simply manifest His love, but **God is love. (1 John 4:18, 16)** The Bible says, **Greater love hath no man than this, that a man lay down his life for his friends. (John 15:13)** If you want to see true and pure love—look at the love of God.

An Unmerited Favor

Even when we were dead in sins, hath quickened us together with Christ, (by grace ye are saved;) (Ephesians 2:5) Grace is just what sinners need. Someone has said, *"Grace is the unmerited inexhaustible supply of God's goodness, making up the difference where we fall short."* Grace is God doing for us that which no one else or nothing else can do for us. Salvation is entirely by grace. **For by grace are ye saved through faith; and that not of yourselves: it is the gift of God: Not of works, lest any man should boast. (Ephesians 2:8-9)** Salvation is always by grace apart from works.

The ultra-dispensationalists would have us to believe that salvation was by grace plus works in the Old Testament and will be by grace plus works in the tribulation. However, such an idea makes God a respecter of persons. God never changes His requirement for salvation. It is the same in the Old and New Testament. The Bible speaks clearly on this matter.

> **But Noah found grace in the eyes of the LORD. (Genesis 6:8)**

> **For if Abraham were justified by works, he hath whereof to glory; but not before God. For what saith the scripture? Abraham believed God, and it**

was counted unto him for righteousness. (Romans 4:2-3)

God is no respecter of persons. He is not going to make the Old Testament saints work for salvation and then give it freely to New Testament saints. Don't miss this important truth. Salvation has always been by grace alone without any mixture of works or merit of our own. **Not by works of righteousness which we have done, but according to his mercy he saved us, by the washing of regeneration, and renewing of the Holy Ghost. (Titus 3:5)** The wonderful grace of God freely works it's miracles in the same life that sin worked it's malice.

An Unrivaled Position

And hath raised us up together, and made us sit together in heavenly places in Christ Jesus. (Ephesians 2:6) What blessed words these are—they speak volumes. Again, Paul speaks of our position in Christ. We are at this very moment **in heavenly places in Christ.** What a change! What a miracle! We have **passed from death unto life. (John 5:24)** The believer is no longer spiritually dead, but spiritually alive. We have been raised from the horrible pit to a heavenly position. Though our locality is here on earth our actual position is in Christ in the Heavens. As believers we exist in two realms. We have a part in two worlds. Our citizenship is in Heaven. **For our conversation is in heaven; from whence also we look for the Saviour, the Lord Jesus Christ. (Philippians 3:20)** While we are citizens of Heaven, we are serving on earth as ambassadors. **Now then we are ambassadors for Christ.... (2 Corinthians 5:20)** An ambassador is one who represents his country in a foreign land. As citizens of Heaven, may we realize that this world is not our home and God help us to live in this strange land as ambassadors representing our Lord Jesus Christ.

An Unending Relationship

That in the ages to come he might shew the exceeding riches of his grace in his kindness toward us through Christ Jesus. (Ephesians 2:7) This verse tells us that it is going to take the **ages to come**, that is; all eternity for God to show us what we have in Christ. The word **shew** comes from *"endeiknymi"* and means *"to display, to demonstrate, to manifest."* We cannot even imagine all the blessings in store for us to experience throughout eternity. **But as it is written, Eye hath not seen, nor ear heard, neither have entered into the heart of man, the things which God hath prepared for them that love him. (1 Corinthians 2:9)** Henry Anderson wrote:

> "How wonderful is that grace which delivers us from such a past, which lifts us up out of a pit so miry, horrible, and poisonous! But God's mercy does not stop at mere deliverance for it raises us up so that we are made to sit with Christ in the heavenlies. Earthly lusts and longings are gone, fetters are broken, for in the heavenly places there is peace, joy, and freedom. But even then grace is not exhausted, for there is opened up an indescribable future summed up in the phrase ages to come."

This not only speaks of our experience in eternity, but also of the fact that we as believers will be part of God's demonstration. His people will be a display of His grace. We will be living trophies of God's grace throughout eternity.

THE CONVERSION OF THE SAINT

Now Paul deals with the saints conversion. These are three very familiar verses that we use often in our witnessing and soul-winning. These verses prove that salvation is by grace alone, that it is the free gift of God.

The Avenue

For by grace are ye saved… (Ephesians 2:8a) The phrase **by grace** has the place of prominence in this passage. It emphasizes the means by which God saves the lost. Grace is God doing for us that which no one else or nothing else can do for us. Salvation is entirely by grace. Grace is God saving a sinner regardless of what he is. Depraved man is full of pride, lies, jealously and idolatry. Many are guilty of adultery, stealing, murder, and all manner of wickedness. But regardless of these and a thousand other sins, God graciously extends His invitation for all men to be saved. That is what makes it grace! It is God's unmerited favor for undeserving sinners. Talk about undeserving! Consider the following verses:

> **For when we were yet without strength, in due time Christ died for the ungodly. (Romans 5:6)**
>
> **But God commendeth his love toward us, in that, while we were yet sinners, Christ died for us. (Romans 5:8)**
>
> **For if, when we were enemies, we were reconciled to God by the death of his Son, much**

more, being reconciled, we shall be saved by his life. (Romans 5:10)

Look at the list of those for whom Jesus paid the penalty of sin. They are described as, **without strength, ungodly, sinners,** and **enemies** of God. What an overwhelming list! A frightening description indeed and it describes every one of us as we were before salvation. **For all have sinned, and come short of the glory of God. (Romans 3:23)** Someone said that God stepped in and made up the difference where we fell short. I disagree! God didn't make up the difference. He did it all. As a result of His grace anyone can enjoy a full and free salvation.

The Agent

Our salvation is by grace, but it is **through faith. (Ephesians 2:8b)** Faith is the means by which salvation becomes a reality in a person's life. However, faith is not a work. It must be understood that the faith is as much the gift of God as the grace. Theodore Epp wrote:

> Because faith is the means of salvation, salvation is placed within the reach of everyone. People have various degrees of faith, but it is not the degree of faith that saves-it is the object of one's faith—Jesus Christ.

By God's grace every person is dealt a measure of faith. **For I say, through the grace given unto me, to every man that is among you, not to think of himself more highly than he ought to think; but to think soberly, according as God hath dealt to every man the measure of faith. (Romans 12:3)** No one is without the ability to exercise saving faith in

Jesus Christ. Upon hearing the plan of salvation an unsaved man has the faith to believe it. God has placed within him a measure of faith and the Word of God has increased that faith. **So then faith cometh by hearing, and hearing by the word of God. (Romans 10:17)**

The Absence

And that not of yourselves: it is the gift of God: Not of works, lest any man should boast. (Ephesians 2:8c-9) Salvation is not by works—it's source is grace and it's means of reception is faith alone. No one will be able to boast that he has done something to earn or aid in obtaining his salvation. **Not by works of righteousness which we have done, but according to his mercy he saved us, by the washing of regeneration, and renewing of the Holy Ghost. (Titus 3:5)** All the glory goes to God for our salvation.

The Action

For we are his workmanship, created in Christ Jesus unto good works, which God hath before ordained that we should walk in them. (Ephesians 2:10) Immediately we notice the fact that salvation changes things. While salvation is apart from works, it is certainly unto works. Notice three great truths here.

First, a **_New Creation_**. We are His **workmanship.** This word **workmanship** comes from the word *"poieoma"* and is used several different ways. It is the word from which we get our English word poem. As a poem expresses the heart of the poet so the Christian is to express the heart of God.

This same word is also used of an artist's painting. Like a painting reflects the artists heart so should the believer's life reflect the heart of God. Someone has well said that "*God has chosen to paint the glory of His grace upon the canvas of our lives.*" The believer's life ought to be lived in such a way that the unsaved world as well other Christians can see that God has done a work in his life. This is the kind of lifestyle that glorifies God.

This word also speaks of a trademark. A trademark is for the purpose of identifying a product with its owner and legally restricting that product to the use of the owner. The Christian is supposed to be displayed as the trademark of God in this world! When the lost world looks at us they are not only to see that we belong to God, but they are to see an example of what God can do with the otherwise ruined life of fallen man.

Second, a ___New Conduct___. We are **created in Christ Jesus unto good works.** God's purpose in saving us goes beyond simply rescuing us from Hell. We quoted Titus 3:5 earlier concerning the fact that our salvation is free and by grace alone. However, when we read a little further we see that God saved us to serve Him. **That being justified by his grace, we should be made heirs according to the hope of eternal life. This is a faithful saying, and these things I will that thou affirm constantly, that they which have believed in God might be careful to maintain good works. These things are good and profitable unto men. (Titus 3:7-8)** Just a little earlier the Bible said that Christ **gave himself for us, that he might redeem us from all iniquity, and purify unto** himself a peculiar people, zealous of good works. (Titus 2:14) We are saved to serve!

Third, a **<u>New Course</u>**. **Which God hath before ordained that we should walk in them.** The word **walk** speaks of lifestyle. Walk is used in the Bible to speak of walking **in newness of life (Romans 6:4),** of walking **after the Spirit (Romans 8:4),** of walking **in honesty (Romans 13:13),** of walking **by faith (2 Corinthians 5:7),** of walking in **good works (Ephesians 2:10),** of walking **in love (Ephesians 5:2),** and of walking **in wisdom. (Colossians 4:5)** The whole idea is that everything changes—even our very lifestyle.

We Are Not What We Were
Ephesians 2:11-22

The Church of Ephesus was predominately made up of Gentile Christians. Notice how Paul begins this section with **Wherefore remember...** He pointed out what they were before God's grace worked in their lives. We shouldn't focus on it, but it does us to remember where we came from. Paul wanted to strengthen their appreciation for God's mercy and grace as well as stir their hearts to a greater love for God. Let us never forget what we were when God saved us from the penalty and power of sin.

WE WERE DESPISED

Wherefore remember, that ye being in time past Gentiles in the flesh, who are called Uncircumcision by that which is called the Circumcision in the flesh made by hands; That at that time ye were without Christ, being aliens from the commonwealth of Israel, and strangers from the covenants of promise, having no hope, and without God in the world. (Ephesians 2:11-12)

We Were Without Circumcision

Wherefore remember, that ye being in time past Gentiles in the flesh, who are called Uncircumcision by that which is called the Circumcision in the flesh made by hands. (Ephesians 2:11) Before Christ, Gentiles were judged racially. The Jews referred to us as the uncircumcised. This was a term of scorn, defamation, and reproach. You will remember that David called Goliath an **uncircumcised Philistine. (1 Samuel 17:26, 36)** It was a derogatory and racial term. There was a very real hatred between the Jews and the Gentiles because of the Jews supposed greatness. Since circumcision was the mark of God's covenant relationship with His people, the Jews considered Gentiles inferior. The Jew was puffed up with pride because of his relationship with God and considered the Gentiles to be of no value or concern to God. Their attitude showed that they had no real concept of circumcision at all. This ritual of circumcision was only a symbol of something deeper. **For he is not a Jew, which is one outwardly; neither is that circumcision, which is outward in the flesh: But he is a Jew, which is one inwardly; and circumcision is that of the heart, in the spirit, and not in the letter; whose praise is not of men, but of God. (Romans 2:28-29)** The circumcision was to be an outward mark of something that had already taken place in the heart.

We Were Without Christ

That at that time ye were without Christ. (Ephesians 2:12a) The promise of the Messiah was given to Israel, not to the Gentiles. Every Old Testament sacrifice pointed to the Messiah. His coming was the desire of every Jew. Gentiles worshipped false gods and knew nothing of a coming Saviour. But praise God, even though Christ came to be Israel's Messiah, He also came to be the world's Saviour.

We Were Without A Commonwealth

We were **aliens from the commonwealth of Israel. (Ephesians 2:12b)** The word **aliens** means "*foreign; not belonging to the same country, land or government;*

Estranged; foreign; not allied; adverse to. That really does not look too good! The word **commonwealth** means *citizenship.* We were on the outside with no entrance, no help, no place to belong.

We Were Without A Covenant

We were **strangers from the covenants of promise... (Ephesians 2:12c)** Gentiles were not the covenant people of God. The Jews alone had a covenant relationship with God. God's covenant with Israel is called the Abrahamic Covenant and is found in Genesis where God said to Abraham, **I will make of thee a great nation, and I will bless thee, and make thy name great; and thou shalt be a blessing: And I will bless them that bless thee, and curse him that curseth thee: and in thee shall all families of the earth be blessed. (Genesis 12:2-3)** Gentiles had no part in these marvelous promises. They were **strangers from the covenants of promise.**

No wonder Paul sums it up by saying that we were without **hope, and without God in the world. (Ephesians 2:12)** To be without hope is a sad and frightening thing. Imagine having to face the fears and the anxieties of life without the hope of Christ's coming. No wonder Paul refers to the rapture as our **blessed hope. (Titus 2:13)** No matter how hard things become we have a blessed hope. However, there are millions out there who know nothing of the Saviour. They are without **hope, and without God in the world.** Can you think of a worse condition? They may have religion, but they are without hope and without God. It is one thing to have religion, but it is quite a different matter to have a personal relationship with God through Christ. Will you give someone the gospel before this week is out?

WE WERE DISTANT

But now in Christ Jesus ye who sometimes were far off are made nigh by the blood of Christ. (Ephesians 2:13) Talk about being distant! Without Christ we were **far off.** The whole human race is a family of bankrupt beggars when it comes to this matter of salvation. Apart from Christ we were **wretched, and miserable, and poor, and blind, and naked. (Revelation 3:17)** We could in no way or by no means pay the price for our salvation. Left to himself, man is helpless, hopeless and lost—doomed to spend eternity in a Devil's Hell. The debt of sin must be paid and the price had to be the life of a Substitute whose blood would cleanse us from all our sins, **for without the shedding of blood there is no remission. (Hebrews 9:22)** Though we were at one time **far off,** we are now **nigh by the blood of Christ.** The shed blood of Jesus was the ransom price. It is only the blood that will pay the sin debt and satisfy the Holy and righteous demands of God, producing peace between Him and sinful man. **Being justified freely by his grace through the redemption that is in Christ Jesus: Whom God hath set forth to be a propitiation through faith in his blood, to declare his righteousness for the remission of sins that are past, through the forbearance of God. (Romans 3:24-25)**

WE WERE DIVIDED

In his fallen state man is helplessly cut off from God. **But your iniquities have separated between you and your God, and your sins have hid his face from you, that he will not hear. (Isaiah 59:2)** So far as our human abilities are concerned there is no way for man to appease the wrath of God and come near to Him. However, Christ has accomplished that which we could not. Notice three things.

The Wall Of Our Separation

For he is our peace, who hath made both one, and hath broken down the middle wall of partition between us; Having abolished in his flesh the enmity, even the law of commandments contained in ordinances; for to make in himself of twain one new man, so making peace. (Ephesians 2:14-15) This verse takes our minds back to the veil of the Temple that separated man from the holy of holies where God dwelt. This veil was torn in two the very moment that Christ died. **Jesus, when he had cried again with a loud voice, yielded up the ghost. And, behold, the veil of the temple was rent in twain from the top to the bottom; and the earth did quake, and the rocks rent. (Matthew 27:50-51)** The rending of the veil in the temple is one of the most significant events surrounding the death of Christ. The veil separated man from the holy of holies where God met the high priest by the mercy seat. Only the high priest could enter there, and he could enter only once a year. It was on the Day of Atonement that the high priest entered the holy of holies to offer blood for his own sins and for the sins of the people. There was sudden and sure death for anyone else who went behind the veil.

The rending of this veil was a Divine act. Notice that the veil was torn in two **from the top to the bottom.** The rending of this veil originated in Heaven. According to Alfred Edersheim, "*The Veil before the Most Holy Place was 40 cubits (60 feet) long, and 20 (30 feet) wide, of the thickness* *of the palm of the hand."* So heavy was this veil that to hang it they had to use two yoke of oxen. The torn veil represented the fact that there was no longer a barrier that separated man from God. Until now only the High Priest was allowed to enter, but since Christ's death man can enter into God's presence.

Notice how Paul uses the word **flesh** here referring to Christ in human form—the work He did on earth. The Old Testament veil pointed to the Lord Jesus Christ. **Having therefore, brethren, boldness to enter into the holiest by the blood of Jesus, By a new and living way, which he hath consecrated for us, through the veil, that is to say, his flesh. (Hebrews 10:19-20)** Here we learn that the veil in the temple was a type of the flesh (the humanity) of the Lord Jesus Christ. The rending of the veil typifies the rending of the flesh of Jesus. Notice that it was at the very moment that Christ died that the veil was torn in two. When Christ died, that which separated man from God (SIN) was paid for and the holy of holies was opened. Now all men became privileged to enter into the presence of God by the precious blood of Jesus Christ. **For there is one God, and one mediator between God and men, the man Christ Jesus. (1 Timothy 2:5)**

The Work Of The Saviour

Having abolished in his flesh the enmity, even the law of commandments contained in ordinances; for to make in himself of twain one new man, so making peace; And that he might reconcile both unto God in one body by the cross, having slain the enmity thereby: And came and preached peace to you which were afar off, and to them that were nigh. (Ephesians 2:15-17) The greatest barrier between the Jew and Gentile was the ceremonial law which Paul refers to as, **the Law of commandments contained in ordinances.** This included the feasts, sacrifices, offerings, and the laws of purification—everything that God commanded of the Jew. Notice that the work of Christ **abolished** these. The word abolished means to *annul; cancel; destroyed* or *to render useless.* We don't have to come to church with a lamb in order to get in. The work of Jesus Christ on the Cross has broken down the barriers and we have access to Him.

The Wooing Of The Spirit

For through him we both have access by one Spirit unto the Father. (Ephesians 2:18) Our union with Christ is by means of the Baptism of the Holy Spirit. It is the Spirit Who draws us to Christ and when we are saved He places us into the family of God. **For by one Spirit are we all baptized into one body, whether we be Jews or Gentiles, whether we be bond or free; and have been all made to drink into one Spirit. (1 Corinthians 12:13)**

WE ARE DELIVERED

Those who are saved have experienced a powerful transition from a condition of enmity and separation to the new and wonderful position in the family of God. We notice three thoughts here.

Our Family

Now therefore ye are no more strangers and foreigners, but fellowcitizens with the saints, and of the household of God. (Ephesians 2:19) We **are no more strangers and**

foreigners. We are no longer **Despised**, **Distant**, and **Divided**—no longer on the outside looking in. We have been **Delivered**! The child of God is not merely saved. Salvation alone is wonderful and far more than we deserve. But on top of that, we have been adopted into the family of God. Adoption is an important New Testament doctrine. **But when the fulness of the time was come, God sent forth his Son, made of a woman, made under the law, To redeem them that were under the law, that we might receive the adoption of sons. (Galatians 4:4-5)** The adoption of the child of God is a powerful and life changing truth. When we adopt a child, the best we can do is give him our name and try to raise and train him for the Lord. Though in every aspect we treat him like a son and love him like our own, we still cannot impart unto him our nature. However, it is quite different with God. God doesn't simply fill out the papers and take us on for support. He literally becomes our Father and we His children. **But as many as received him, to them gave he power to become the sons of God, even to them that believe on his name. (John 1:12)** As God's children we are not just placed into the family, we literally become **partakers of the divine nature. (2 Peter 1:4)**

The word **adoption** as used in the Word of God comes from a word that literally means *son-placed* or *the making of a son.* It is a legal term speaking of our official position in Christ. We have all of the privileges and rights that come with sonship. **For ye have not received the spirit of bondage again to fear; but ye have received the Spirit of adoption, whereby we cry, Abba, Father. The Spirit itself beareth witness with our spirit, that we are the children of God: And if children, then heirs; heirs of God, and joint-**

heirs with Christ; if so be that we suffer with him, that we may be also glorified together. (Romans 8:15-17) As children we are placed into the family of God with full rights and privileges. So much so that we can address God as Abba, Father. The word **Abba** is the Aramaic word for *Father.* It is similar to the English word *Daddy,* a term of endearment used by small children in addressing their fathers. Jesus used this term when praying in the garden of Gethsemane. **And he said, Abba, Father, all things are possible unto thee; take away this cup from me: nevertheless not what I will, but what thou wilt. (Mark 14:36)** What a precious relationship we have with God. We are His children, so much so that we are joint-heirs with Christ.

Our Foundation

And are built upon the foundation of the apostles and prophets, Jesus Christ himself being the chief corner stone. (Ephesians 2:20) A structure will not last unless it is built upon a solid foundation. Here we learn that the household of God is built upon a solid and sure foundation. Paul said:

> **According to the grace of God which is given unto me, as a wise masterbuilder, I have laid the foundation, and another buildeth thereon. But let every man take heed how he buildeth thereupon. For other foundation can no man lay than that is laid, which is Jesus Christ. (1 Corinthians 3:10-11)**

The apostles were Christ's instruments in building the early Church. Notice that Christ is the **chief corner stone.**

The apostles didn't start the Church, they simply built upon that which Christ started as we do today.

<u>Our Framing</u>

In whom all the building fitly framed together groweth unto an holy temple in the Lord: In whom ye also are builded together for an habitation of God through the Spirit. (Ephesians 2:21-22) This verse speaks of the unity of the body. We are to be **fitly framed together.** This is a builder's term that carries the idea of the *careful joining of every part of a piece of furniture or building.* Each piece of wood has to be precisely cut and then many times trimmed and sanded to get the right fit and finish. This is the picture that God uses of us. Everyone who comes to Christ is taken by God and **fitly framed** into the proper place in the building. Notice also that we are not just a bunch of brothers and sisters sharing a house. We are the **habitation of God.** God lives with us! What a family!

A Mystery Revealed
Ephesians 3:1-13

For this cause... The words for this cause (3:1) connect the previous two chapters with what Paul is about to say. Paul's **cause** was the great salvation truths of chapters one and two. Paul takes those great truths and builds upon them, instructing the Ephesians concerning God's plan for the Church from ages past.

THE PRISONER

For this cause I Paul, the prisoner of Jesus Christ for you Gentiles. (Ephesians 3:1) Three times in the book of Ephesians, Paul refers to himself as a prisoner (3:1, 4:1, and in 6:20 in bonds). Paul wrote this letter while he was imprisoned in Rome. However, take note of how Paul viewed his status as a prisoner. Though in jail for 5 years (2 in Caesarea and 3 in Rome), Paul did not view himself a prisoner of the Jews, Rome, or Caesar. He called himself a **prisoner of Jesus Christ.** A prisoner is one who has been captured and detained. Such was the case with Paul. His heart had been captured by Christ.

THE PIONEER

Paul was more than a prisoner, he was a pioneer going where no man had ever gone before. He was taking the message of God's grace to the Gentiles. Never before had the message of God grace been offered to the Gentiles. However, when the Jews rejected Christ (John 1:11), God opened the door to the Gentiles (Romans 11).

It Was A Dispensational Message

If ye have heard of the dispensation of the grace of God which is given me to you-ward: (Ephesians 3:2) The word **dispensation** is the Greek word *"oikonomia."* It was a word that was used to describe the management of a household. The idea is that of a steward or an administrator. A steward or an administrator is the manager of another's affairs. In the United States we have administrations. When a new President is elected, he sets up a new administration. That new administration manages the affairs of the country until a new president is elected. Each administration lasts between four and eight years. God works in a similar way. He also has dispensations in which He deals with man. There are seven dispensations in the Word of God.

1. ***Dispensation of Innocence***. The first dispensation ran from the creation of man (Genesis 1:26-28; 2:7) to their removal from Eden. (Genesis 3:23,24)

2. ***Dispensation of Conscience***. The second dispensation began with mans fall and removal from the garden and ends with the Flood. During this dispensation man was without law and under conscience.

3. ***Dispensation of Human Government***. The third dispensation began with the judgment of the Flood of Noah's day. God saved eight people—Noah, his wife, and his three sons along with their wives. God at this time instituted Human Government. During this time men were to govern themselves.

4. ***Dispensation of Promise***. The fourth dispensation began with the call of Abram and lasted until the giving of the Law at Sinai. God promised to Abram personal blessings: an earthly and spiritual blessing; the land of Canaan for a possession, and an innumerable seed through which the nation would be blessed.

5. ***Dispensation of the Law***. The fifth dispensation extended from the giving of the Law at Sinai to the coming of Christ. Up to this time God had called and anointed men. Now, God chooses and sets apart a nation for His glory—the nation Israel.

6. ***Dispensation of Grace***. It is in this sixth dispensation that we are living now. During this dispensation God is a calling out a bride. There is no distinction made between Jew and Gentile. All have sinned and come short of the glory of God. All are guilty before God and hopelessly lost in their sin. God is calling whosoever will to come and be saved.

7. ***Dispensation Of The Kingdom***. The seventh dispensation will follow the judgment of the nations and close with the loosing of Satan at the end of the Millennium. (Revelation 20:7) It will run for one thousand years. (Revelation 20:2,3) During this time, the seat of government will be Jerusalem. (Isaiah 24:23) Jesus will sit on the throne; (Luke 1:32-33) and the saved will reign with Him (Revelation 20:6) over Israel and all the earth.

A **dispensation of the grace of God** had been given to Paul. He told the Romans, **For I speak to you Gentiles, inasmuch as I am the apostle of the Gentiles, I magnify** mine office. **(Romans 11:13)** God had entrusted Paul with the gospel of Jesus Christ and he had the responsibility to take it to the Gentiles.

It Was Divine Message

How that by revelation he made known unto me the mystery; (as I wrote afore in few words, Whereby, when ye read, ye may understand my knowledge in the mystery of Christ). (Ephesians 3:3-4) Paul received his stewardship by Divine **revelation**. He didn't pick it up at some conference or from the pages of a book. Paul was acting with Divine authority.

The word **mystery** speaks of that which was previously unknown. In the New Testament it refers to the doctrine which is specific for the Church Age. It is called **the mystery** because it's truths were never revealed in Old Testament Scriptures.

Which in other ages was not made known unto the sons of men, as it is now revealed unto his holy apostles and prophets by the Spirit. (Ephesians 3:5) The great truths that had not been revealed to the Old Testament saints were now being revealed to the Gentiles by Paul and are still being revealed today through the preaching and propagation of the gospel.

It Was A Delightful Message

That the Gentiles should be fellowheirs, and of the same body, and partakers of his promise in Christ by the gospel. (Ephesians 3:6) No longer is the message of salvation for a select nation, but for whosoever will. Jesus said, **salvation is of the Jews. (John 4:22)** Before Christ, if a person wanted to be saved, he had to approach God through the Jews. However, since Christ, all the peoples of the earth can come directly to God through Jesus Christ. **For there is one God, and one mediator between God and men, the man Christ Jesus. (1 Timothy 2:5)** No longer do we have to approach God through any other people or religion—we have direct access to God through Jesus Christ.

THE PREACHING

Paul was sent to **preach among the Gentiles. (3:8)** Preaching is God's method of propagating the gospel. The command **Preach the word... (2 Timothy 4:2)** stands at the forefront. We Baptists believe in the primacy of preaching— that preaching is supreme. **How then shall they call on him in whom they have not believed? and how shall they believe in him of whom they have not heard? and how shall they hear without a preacher? (Romans 10:14)** Paul took his duty seriously. A study of Paul's life reveals that he was faithful to his call of spreading the gospel of Christ.

Paul's Help

Whereof I was made a minister, according to the gift of the grace of God given unto me by the effectual working of his power. (Ephesians 3:7) Paul realized that he was **made a minister**. Paul didn't just decide one day to serve in the ministry. He was a God made minister. The word **minister** comes from the word *"diakonos"* and refers to a servant. It describes one who waits on and serves another. Paul wasn't a big shot, he was a servant.

Paul's work was **according to the gift of the grace of God.** Preaching and teaching were Paul's spiritual gifts. Grace is unmerited favor. Paul didn't have any innate qualities that made him a candidate for the ministry. It was just the opposite. He was hostile toward Christ and His people. But God's grace made the difference.

God took Paul and **made** him a minister by the **effectual working of his power.** It wasn't Paul's education. It wasn't his experience. It had nothing to do with his expertise. It was solely by the enabling of God. The operating power for the ministry comes from the omnipotent God of Heaven. Nothing else will do. Thank God for education, experience and expertise. But worldly professions have all of this. The difference is the power of God. If we are going to be servants who please the Master, we must have His enabling.

Paul's Humility

Unto me, who am less than the least of all saints, is this grace given ... (Ephesians 3:8a) Paul was humbled by the fact that God would use him in the gospel ministry. Paul saw himself as **less than the least of all saints.** Paul's recognition of God's grace and enabling helped to keep him humble. One of the greatest dangers that a preacher faces is pride. It seems that as God blesses us we have the tendency to start thinking more highly of ourselves than we ought. Paul always kept this in mind.

> **For I am the least of the apostles, that am not meet to be called an apostle, because I persecuted the church of God. But by the grace of God I am what I am: and his grace which was bestowed upon me was not in vain; but I laboured more abundantly than they all: yet not I, but the grace of God which was with me. (1 Corinthians 15:9-10)**

Even though Paul was chosen to be an apostle, minister to the Gentiles and to know and reveal mysteries, he still considered himself to be the least of all the saints. This was not false humility. It was the heart of the Paul.

Paul's Herald

That I should preach among the Gentiles the unsearchable riches of Christ; (Ephesians 3:8b) The word **preach comes from** *"euangelizo"* and means *"to announce good news."* Good news indeed! God has reached out to the Gentiles. Paul says, **And to make all men see what is the fellowship of the mystery, which from the beginning of the world hath been hid in God, who created all things by Jesus Christ. (Ephesians 3:9)** The mystery had been revealed and Paul was consumed with his calling to get the truth to men. The word **unsearchable** in verse eight comes from a word that means *"not tracked out, untraceable, past finding out."* It is a word that describes something so deep and so vast that it is beyond finding out. It is something so deep that you can explore for a lifetime without getting to the bottom. The riches of Christ cannot be exhausted, but it is the preachers work to declare those riches to the lost as well as the saved.

THE PURPOSE

To the intent that now unto the principalities and powers in heavenly places might be known by the church the manifold wisdom of God, According to the eternal purpose which he purposed in Christ Jesus our Lord: (Ephesians 3:10-11) These principalities and powers in heavenly places are the angels of God. Even though these angels were in the presence of God, they did not know about the mystery of the Church. God saving Jews and Gentiles and uniting them in one body revealed to the angels His manifold wisdom. This all was according to the **eternal purpose** which God brought to fruition in Jesus Christ.

THE PERSEVERANCE

In whom we have boldness and access with confidence by the faith of him. Wherefore I desire that ye faint not at my tribulations for you, which is your glory. (Ephesians 3:12-13) As Believers in Christ we can now go boldly before God. **Let us therefore come boldly unto the throne of grace, that we may obtain mercy, and find grace to help in time of need. (Hebrews 4:16)** Not only are we allowed to come before God, but we have complete access to Him.

How To Pray For The Brethren
Ephesians 3:14-21

For this cause I bow my knees unto the Father of our Lord Jesus Christ, Of whom the whole family in heaven and earth is named, (Ephesians 3:14-15) Up to this point Paul has laid out some of the great truths of the Christian life. He has explained who we are in Christ, the way of salvation, and our unlimited riches and resources. Now Paul prays that the Ephesian believers would comprehend the truth of what he has said and enjoy the benefits of salvation. There are five specific things that Paul prays for here.

A POWERFUL ENABLING

That he would grant you, according to the riches of his glory... (Ephesians 3:16a) Paul prays for God to strength according to the riches of his glory. Man usually gives out of his riches rather than according to his riches. If a millionaire gives a $ 100.00 to charity, he is giving out of his riches. But if he give $ 200,000.00, he is giving according to his riches. The greater the wealth, the greater the gift must be in order to qualify as giving according to his riches. For God to give according to His riches is far beyond our ability to comprehend. God's riches are limitless. Yet that is exactly the standard by which Paul asks God to empower believers.

... to be strengthened with might by his Spirit in the inner man; (Ephesians 3:16b) The word **might** is from the Greek *"dynamis"* and means power. If we are to excel in the Christian life we must be strengthened by his Spirit in the inner man. Of our own selves we are absolutely powerless to accomplish our spiritual responsibilities. Jesus said, **the flesh profiteth nothing: (John 6:63)** Now notice that the emphasis here is strength for the **inner man**. It is the spiritual part of man that Paul is talking about here. Now the outer man, we take fairly good care of him. We feed him, we bathe him and we dress him up. And for what? Where is he headed? Paul says ... **our outward man perish. (2 Corinthians 4:16)** The word **perish** means to *"decay, corrupt, destroy."* Webster says, *"to die; to lose life in any manner ... to wither and decay .. to waste."* Many Christians sadly pay more attention to the **outward** than they do the **inward**. But God especially focuses on the inward. The Christian life is lived from the heart—from the inside out. It is the Spirit of God Who furnishes the strength to live the Christian life. **Not by might, nor by power, but by my spirit, saith the LORD of hosts. (Zechariah 4:6)**

A PERSONAL ENTHRONEMENT

That Christ may dwell in your hearts by faith;... (Ephesians 3:17a) The verb **dwell** means to *"to reside."* It carries the idea of settling down and feeling at home. Christ indwells every believer. The Bible says ... **Christ in you, the hope of glory: (Colossians 1:27)** While Christ indwells every believer the question is: "Does Christ feel at home?" Too often believers treat Christ more like a visitor than a resident. Paul wants Christ to feel at home in the believer's life. This is not a causal relationship, but an intimate one.

A PERMANENT ESTABLISHMENT

... that ye, being rooted and grounded in love, (Ephesians 3:17b) Paul's uses picturesque language as he prays for believers to be established. The word **rooted** is an agricultural term that speaks of a tree firmly rooted and drawing nourishment from the soil. The word **grounded** is an architectural term and speaks the foundation of a building. For any structure to be safe and secure, the foundation must be solid. A Christian is who is rooted and grounded in love will be stable and sustained.

A PRECIOUS EXPERIENCE

May be able to comprehend with all saints what is the breadth, and length, and depth, and height; (Ephesians 3:18) The word **comprehend** means *"to lay hold of, to seize."* It carries the idea of having a firm grasp on something. Paul wanted believers to get a hold of what God's love. Paul lists four dimensions of God's love.

Breadth speaks of the width and suggests God love is all encompassing. God's love is wide enough to save whosoever will.

Length speaks of the duration of God's love. God never stops loving. In Romans Paul asked the question Who shall separate us from the love of Christ? (Romans 8:35) He goes on to show that nothing or no one can curve God's love for us.

The **depth** of God's love is seen the fact that He gave His only begotten Son to save lost man. The depth of God's love is fathomless.

The **height** of God's love reaches to the heavens. This is the very home of God from which every believer is blessed (Ephesians 1:3).

And to know the love of Christ, which passeth knowledge ... (Ephesians 3:19a) Paul wants us to know the love of Christ but notice that His love **passeth knowledge.** His love is beyond our ability to comprehend. The word

know comes from the Greek *"ginosko"* and means *"to be aware of, to perceive, to understand."* It carries the idea of having an experiential knowledge. The human mind cannot fully understand God's love, but we can experience it. Paul has just stated the fact of the **breadth, and length, and depth, and height** of God's love. Now he prays for the believer enter into and experiment that love.

PLEASING ENRICHMENT

... that ye might be filled with all the fulness of God. (Ephesians 3:19b) The word **filled** comes from *"pleroo"* and means *"to make full."* When a glass is full there is no room for anything else. That is the picture here. Paul prays that God would flood the believer's life with His fullness. When a Christian is filled in this way, he is totally controlled by God.

Now unto him that is able to do exceeding abundantly above all that we ask or think, according to the power that worketh in us, (Ephesians 3:20) The Omnipotent God operates in a realm that is far beyond our ability to even understand. The phrase **exceeding abundantly above** carries the idea of *"beyond all measure and infinitely more."* What limitless power! God is **able** to make the believer the kind of Christian that Paul has just prayed we would be. The Holy Spirit is **the power that worketh in us.** The Holy Spirit dwells in the believer. But He is not hanging around and just sitting there—He is working within us.

Unto him be glory in the church by Christ Jesus throughout all ages, world without end. Amen. (Ephesians 3:21) Praise and glory rightfully and properly belongs to God. Paul's greatest desire was that Christ be glorified through the believer.

The Worthy Walk
Ephesians 4:1-6

The word **walk** speaks of lifestyle. Walk is used in the Bible to speak of walking **in newness of life (Romans 6:4),** of walking **after the Spirit (Romans 8:4),** of walking **in honesty (Romans 13:13),** of walking **by faith (2 Corinthians 5:7),** of walking in **good works (Ephesians 2:10),** of walking **in love (Ephesians 5:2),** and of walking **in wisdom. (Colossians 4:5)** The whole idea is this: If we are going to be an example of the gospel we must be different from the world. As the old saying goes, "Our walk must match our talk."

THE CALL TO THE WORTHY WALK

I therefore, the prisoner of the Lord, beseech you that ye walk worthy of the vocation wherewith ye are called. (Ephesians 4:1) Every believer is called to a worthy walk. Paul made a similar appeal to the believers at Colosse.

> **For this cause we also, since the day we heard it, do not cease to pray for you, and to desire that ye might be filled with the knowledge of his will in all wisdom and spiritual understanding; That ye might walk worthy of the Lord unto all pleasing, being fruitful in every good work, and increasing in the knowledge of God. (Colossians 1:9-10)**

The word **worthy** comes from the Greek *"axios."* It is a very graphic word meaning *"a balance* or *having the weight of another thing."* It speaks of the bartering system of the ancient world where a range of weights were used to determine the weight and value of an item. Paul uses the analogy of the balance to emphasize a great truth. On one side of the scale is our calling and on the other side is our life. The bottom line is that a believer's life is to balance out with God's calling.

> **For God hath not called us unto uncleanness, but unto holiness. (1 Thessalonians 4:7)**

> **Who hath saved us, and called *us* with an holy calling, not according to our works, but according to his own purpose and grace, which was given us in Christ Jesus before the world began, (2 Timothy 1:9)**

Our life is to be worthy of our calling. Our life is to balance out with God's expectation. One whose Lips profess Christianity is to have a Life that professes the same. The idea is to make sure that our walk matches our talk.

THE CHARACTERISTICS OF THE WORTHY WALK

With all lowliness and meekness, with longsuffering, forbearing one another in love. (Ephesians 4:2) Paul begins to spell out some of the characteristics of a worthy walk.

Lowliness

Lowliness is defined by Noah Webster as *"freedom from pride; humility; humbleness of mind."* **Lowliness** is the opposite of pride. **Likewise, ye younger, submit yourselves unto the elder. Yea, all of you be subject one to another, and be clothed with humility: for God resisteth the proud, and giveth grace to the humble. Humble yourselves therefore under the mighty hand of God, that he may exalt you in due time. (1 Peter 5:5-6)** Pride is at work when we exalt ourselves. Humility is at work when God exalts us.

Webster defines pride as, *Inordinate self-esteem; an unreasonable conceit of one's own superiority in talents, beauty, wealth, accomplishments, rank or elevation in office, which manifests itself in lofty airs, distance, reserve, and often in contempt of others.* It is unacceptable for Christians to go around boasting of their abilities and accomplishments as if God were lucky to have them. We expect such foolishness from the world, but not from God's people.

Paul considered himself to be **less than the least of all saints. (Ephesians 3:8)** Such humility comes only from an intimate relationship with God. This is the attitude of a truly great man. This wasn't a false humility, but the consistent attitude of Paul. **But by the grace of God I am what I am: and his grace which was bestowed upon me was not in vain; but I laboured more abundantly than they all: yet not I, but the grace of God which was with me. (1 Corinthians 15:10)** Paul, who had once been a proud Pharisee, was now a humble child of God. One of the characteristics of the worthy walk is lowliness.

Longsuffering

The next two characteristics, meekness and longsuffering, both describe the gentle patience of the believer.

The word **meekness** basically means *"mild, gentle, or softness of temper."* Meekness is not weakness or a lack of power. Rather, it is power under control. An ox has tremendous power, but in the yoke is under control and able to be turned in any direction by the will of it's master. Jesus is the perfect example of meekness. **Take my yoke upon you, and learn of me; for I am meek and lowly in heart: and ye shall find rest unto your souls. (Matthew 11:29)**

Meekness is the strength to control and discipline one's self. Meekness is a necessary requirement for reaching and dealing with people.

> **In meekness instructing those that oppose themselves; if God peradventure will give them repentance to the acknowledging of the truth. (2 Timothy 2:25)**

It is a requirement for restoring the fallen.

> **Brethren, if a man be overtaken in a fault, ye which are spiritual, restore such an one in the spirit of meekness; considering thyself, lest thou also be tempted. (Galatians 6:1)**

The word **longsuffering** simply means to suffer long. It speaks of patience and endurance under affliction and provocation. The word carrics the idea of restraint, patience and endurance, of mistreatment without anger or thought of revenge. That is a hard thing to accomplish in the flesh. The flesh seeks revenge. When the old flesh says, *"retaliate,"* longsuffering says, *"Love them, that is what Christ would do."* Longsuffering is one of God's attributes. **But thou, O Lord, art a God full of compassion, and gracious, longsuffering, and plenteous in mercy and truth. (Psalm 86:15)** If we live a Spirit filled life, we too will be longsuffering even under mistreatment.

The most beautiful picture of longsuffering comes from the life of Jesus Christ. At the crucifixion He could have summoned **more than twelve legions of angels (Matthew 26:53)** to His side to defend Him, but instead, He **endured the cross. (Hebrews 12:2)** Later He prayed for their forgiveness. **Then said Jesus, Father, forgive them; for they**

know not what they do. And they parted his raiment, and cast lots. (Luke 23:34) That's longsuffering!

Love

Forbearing one another in love. Noah Webster defines **forbearing** as a *"ceasing or restraining from action."* It is a love that continues to love even under mistreatment. **Charity suffereth long, and is kind. (1 Corinthians 13:4)** Peter put it this way. **And above all things have fervent charity among yourselves: for charity shall cover the multitude of sins. (1 Peter 4:8)** Forbearing love covers the sins of others, not to justify or excuse them, but to exercise the grace necessary to deal with the sinner.

Love is another characteristic of those who walk worthy of their calling. It is a love that comes from God. **For God so loved the world, that he gave his only begotten Son, that whosoever believeth in him should not perish, but have everlasting life. (John 3:16)** The greatest demonstration of love this world has ever known is the cross of Calvary. The evidence of His unwavering love is the sacrifice of His Son for the sin of a lost world. **But God commendeth his love toward us, in that, while we were yet sinners, Christ died for us. (Romans 5:8)** Christ's death demonstrated God's unconditional love for us. Calvary's cross is the undeniable proof of God's love.

Love is listed as a fruit of the Spirit. **But the fruit of the Spirit is love…. (Galatians 5:22a)** True biblical love is more than mere lip service. Real love demands sacrifice and commitment. **Hereby perceive we the love of God, because he laid down his life for us: and we ought to lay down our lives for the brethren. (1 John 3:16)** The demands of

Biblical love go far beyond cheap words. **But whoso hath this world's good, and seeth his brother have need, and shutteth up his bowels of compassion from him, how dwelleth the love of God in him?. (1 John 3:17)** Biblical love knows no boundaries—it is a sacrificial love. When the Holy Spirit has control of our lives He reproduces that same love in us. **The love of God is shed abroad in our hearts by the Holy Ghost which is given unto us. (Romans 5:5b)**

THE CLOSENESS OF THE WORTHY WALK

Endeavouring to keep the unity of the Spirit in the bond of peace. (Ephesians 4:3) Paul declares that unity in the local Church is hard work. We are to be **Endeavouring to keep the unity.** The word **endeavouring** comes from the Greek *"spoudazo"* and means to *"make every effort and to work hard at maintaining."* Unity doesn't just happen because we are saved—we have to work at it. Unity is important if we are to accomplish our goal of reaching the world with the gospel. Paul exhorted the Philippian believers, **Only let your conversation be as it becometh the gospel of Christ: that whether I come and see you, or else be absent, I may hear of your affairs, that ye stand fast in one spirit, with one mind striving together for the faith of the gospel. (Philippians 1:27)** Notice how Paul stressed the importance of unity with the words **stand fast in one spirit.** The words **one spirit** carries the idea of being united as *one soul.* Every local Church needs unity. The early Christians in the book of Acts were of **one accord (Acts 1:14; 2:1; 2:46; 4:24; 15:25).** No wonder there was such a mighty moving of God in those days.

Paul goes on to drive the ball home. He exhorted the Philippian believers to be **striving together for the faith of**

the gospel. The word **striving** is from the Greek *"athleoo"* and carries the idea of contending in an athletic event. It speaks of a teamwork whereby a group of athletes pull together and give it their all to defeat a common foe and win the game. Paul compares the church to a team of athletes, and admonishes them that it is teamwork that wins the victory.

Certainly there can be no unity between those who hold to the Word of God, and modernistic liberals who deny the precious truths of God's Word. Alliances with such men will only weaken the believer. Our instruction concerning that crowd is clear. **Bc ye not unequally yoked together... (2 Corinthians 6:14a)** We are commanded to **...have no fellowship with the unfruitful works of darkness, but rather reprove them. (Ephesians 5:11)** However, while there will never be a Biblical unity between Bible believers and liberals, there can and should be a precious unity among those of **like precious faith. (2 Peter 1:1)** This will be a unity like that in the early Church. **And the multitude of them that believed were of one heart and of one soul: neither said any of them that ought of the things which he possessed was his own; but they had all things common. (Acts 4:32)** Without such cooperation and unity among believers the work of God suffers. **Behold, how good and how pleasant it is for brethren to dwell together in unity! (Psalm 133:1)**

THE CAUSE OF THE WORTHY WALK

There is one body, and one Spirit, even as ye are called in one hope of your calling; One Lord, one faith, one baptism, One God and Father of all, who is above all, and through all, and in you all. (Ephesians 4:4-6) Having made the appeal for believers to walk worthy, endeavoring to keep the unity of the Spirit, Paul goes on to list the seven-fold basis of spiritual unity among believers.

One Body

There is **one body. (Ephesians 4:4a)** This refers to the family of God where every believer is placed immediately upon conversion (1 Corinthians 12:13). All genuine believers in the Lord Jesus Christ are blood kin brothers and sisters. The ground is level at the cross. Regardless of race, nationality, culture, age, education, and social position, all are the same in Christ. Praise God for His wonderful salvation. The Word of God clearly teaches that all who have placed their faith in Jesus Christ are born again believers and members of the family of God. While we may not agree with every detail of their denominational beliefs, we are obligated, nonetheless, as Christians to live by His grace and, to treat them as brethren. Paul said, **If it be possible, as much as lieth in you, live peaceably with all men. (Romans 12:18)**

This being said, it must be understood that this is no excuse for an unequal yoke. Our fellowship is only as long as we can do so without compromising our convictions or sacrificing our loyalty to our Lord and Saviour and His Word. Any time we are required to compromise fundamental doctrine we must separate.

One Spirit

There is **one Spirit. (Ephesians 4:4b)** Jesus said, **That which is born of the flesh is flesh; and that which is born of the Spirit is spirit. (John 3:6)** It is through the ministry of the Holy Spirit that the Christ life begins and is continued. Every born again believer has the Spirit of God permanently living in his life. **But ye are not in the flesh, but in the Spirit, if so be that the Spirit of God dwell in you. Now if any man have not the Spirit of Christ, he is none of his. (Romans 8:9)** What a precious miracle! Upon a person placing faith in Jesus Christ the Holy Spirit regenerates his soul and transforms him into a new creature in Christ Jesus. **Except a man be born of water and of the Spirit, he cannot enter into the kingdom of God. That which is born of the flesh is flesh; and that which is born of the Spirit is spirit. (John 3:5-6)** Peter wrote, **Whereby are given unto us exceeding great and precious promises: that by these ye might be partakers of the divine nature, having escaped the corruption that is in the world through lust. (2 Peter 1:4)** The new nature is given to man as the result of being born again. **Therefore if any man be in Christ, he is a new creature: old things are passed away; behold, all things are become new. (2 Corinthians 5:17)** The new nature cannot and will not sin because it is born of God. **Whosoever is born of God doth not commit sin; for his seed remaineth in him: and he cannot sin, because he is born of God. (1 John 3:9)** When the believer sins it is because he submits and succumbs to the old nature. However, as we submit to the Holy Spirit and live according to the new nature we enjoy victory and success in the Christian life. If every believer were to live according to the dictates of the Holy Spirit there would be harmony among God's people.

One Hope

There is **one hope. (Ephesians 4:4c)** All believers have a common hope. It is the rapture when Christ will return to gather us to Himself. **Looking for that blessed hope, and the glorious appearing of the great God and our Saviour Jesus Christ (Titus 2:13)** This is something that we are to be looking for. The rapture of the Christian is indeed our wonderful and blessed hope. Every true child of God today has this hope.

> **For the Lord himself shall descend from heaven with a shout, with the voice of the archangel, and with the trump of God; and the dead in Christ shall rise first; Then we which are alive and remain shall be caught up together with them in the clouds, to meet the Lord in the air: and so shall we ever be with the Lord. (1 Thessalonians 4:16-17)**

This great event known as the rapture is the next great event in the redemptive plan and purpose of God. Our Lord will return literally and visibly, and summon His people with a shout like a trumpet blast. The grave of every dead saint will give up its dead and those still living at that time will be **caught up** with Christ to ever be with Him. Jesus said, **In my Father's house are many mansions: if it were not so, I would have told you. I go to prepare a place for you. And if I go and prepare a place for you, I will come again, and receive you unto myself; that where I am, there ye may be also. (John 14:2-3)** What a wonderful hope!

One Lord

There is **one Lord. (Ephesians 4:5a)** The Bible places great emphasis on the Lordship of Jesus Christ. Read the gospels and note how that nearly every time someone came to Christ the title Lord is used. It is a sad time among

Christians when there has to be a debate concerning the Lordship of Christ. However, in the New Testament, there is no such thing as salvation or victory apart from Christ's Lordship. The word **Lord** comes from the Greek *"kyrios"* and means *"supreme in authority."* The idea is that of a Master over his servants. The household of faith has one Master, one Lord—the Lord Jesus Christ.

One Faith

There is **one faith. (Ephesians 4:5b)** The phrase **one faith** speaks of the entire revelation from God, the whole body of truth as contained in His Word. Men throughout the ages have attempted to add to and take away from the body of doctrine. Such activity has only resulted in disunity and accounts for the great number of denominations and cults that are present today. So important is this body of truth that we are commanded to **... earnestly contend for the faith which was once delivered unto the saints. (Jude 1:3)** The words **earnestly contend** comes from the Greek *"epagonizomai"* and means *"to strive against; to struggle in opposition."* Militarily it speaks of a strenuous, intense, determined struggle to conquer the enemy.

The Christian life is a war in which we must daily contend with the enemy. In the book of Ephesians Paul likened the Christian life to that of a soldier on a battlefield. **For we wrestle not against flesh and blood, but against principalities, against powers, against the rulers of the darkness of this world, against spiritual wickedness in high places. (Ephesians 6:12)** The primary feature of our conflict with Satan is defensive. It is all out war as we contend against the forces of evil. Notice that Paul uses such terms as **stand**, **wrestle** and **withstand** to describe the intensity of our conflict.

One Baptism

There is **one baptism. (Ephesians 4:5c)** This whole list deals with the spiritual, not physical or organizational. Therefore I see no need to attempt to interpret this as water baptism. **For by one Spirit are we all baptized into one body, whether we be Jews or Gentiles, whether we be bond or free; and have been all made to drink into one Spirit. (1 Corinthians 12:13)** This takes place at the moment of salvation when the Holy Spirit places the believer into the family of God.

One God

There is **One God and Father of all, who is above all, and through all, and in you all. (4:6)** Paul once again emphasizes the fact of our family standing. All Christians belong together as brothers and sisters, and share the conviction that God is their Father. He is the Father and we are the children.

The Giver And His Gifts
Ephesians 4:7-16

I heard of a Pastor who said his Church was a 100% willing when it came to work. And then explained 20% were willing to do all the work and the other 80% were willing to let them. If a Church operates that way it will never reach its potential for Christ. Just imagine the impact that a Church would have if it were operating at 100% efficiency. God has given us gifts for the work of the ministry so that we can operate at peak efficiency.

THE GRANTEE

But unto every one of us is given grace according to the measure of the gift of Christ. (Ephesians 4:7) Having just taught on unity of the body, Paul now explains that there is a diversity of gifts and positions within the body. Notice the words, **every one of us is given...** There is not one single believer who is passed over or left out. Every child of God is given a distinctive gift by which he or she is to serve God in the local body.

> **Now there are diversities of gifts, but the same Spirit. And there are differences of administrations, but the same Lord. And there are diversities of operations, but it is the same God which worketh all in all. But the manifestation of the Spirit is given to every man to profit withal. (1 Corinthians 12:4-7)**

> **Having then gifts differing according to the grace that is given to us, whether prophecy, let us prophesy according to the proportion of faith; Or**

ministry, let us wait on our ministering: or he that teacheth, on teaching; Or he that exhorteth, on exhortation: he that giveth, let him do it with simplicity; he that ruleth, with diligence; he that showeth mercy, with cheerfulness. (Romans 12:6-8)

To each believer there is **given grace according to the measure of the gift of Christ. (Ephesians 4:7b)** This is not saving grace, this is serving grace. This is Christ's enabling of the believer to serve in the capacity and manner in which he has been called. Paul spoke earlier of such grace. **Whereof I was made a minister, according to the gift of the grace of God given unto me by the effectual working of his power. Unto me, who am less than the least of all saints, is this grace given, that I should preach among the Gentiles the unsearchable riches of Christ. (Ephesians 3:7-8)** The fact that it is by grace implies that it has nothing to do with our own abilities. No one can boast about his accomplishments for Christ. The only thing we can say is, "Praise God! To God be the glory!"

THE GIVER

Wherefore he saith, When he ascended up on high, he led captivity captive, and gave gifts unto men. (Now that he ascended, what is it but that he also descended first into the lower parts of the earth? He that descended is the same also that ascended up far above all heavens, that he might fill all things). (Ephesians 4:8-10) Here is the illustration of a king who has been victorious in battle. He has conquered his enemy and is returning home in glory. The king is riding upon his white stallion, following is his army—his faithful soldiers. Behind them comes the captured enemy soldiers shackled in chains, defeated and helpless. Paul is quoting part of Psalm 68:18, one of David's victories, as an illustration. David had liberated a number of captives who had been taken out of Israel. He brought those captives back in triumph and in victory to reunite them with their families and their homeland. David captured those who were in captivity and brought them home. Paul takes that historical account and uses it as an illustration of Christ's victorious ascension. He also uses the same illustration in Colossians in speaking of Christ's victory over the principalities and powers of darkness. **And having spoiled principalities and powers, he made a show of them openly, triumphing over them in it. (Colossians 2:15)** When Christ ascended up on high, He did so as a mighty and victorious King.

Notice that Jesus **also descended first into the lower parts of the earth. (Ephesians 4:9b)** During the New Testament times when a believer died he enters immediately into the presence of God. **For I am in a strait betwixt two, having a desire to depart, and to be with Christ; which is far better. (Philippians 1:23)** Paul spoke of death as departing and being with Christ. Later he said, **We are confident, I say, and willing rather to be absent from the body, and to be present with the Lord. (2 Corinthians 5:8)** Clearly the New Testament teaches that those who die in Christ go immediately to be with Him.

However, in the Old Testament that was not the case. We see this clearly in Jesus' teaching on the rich man and Lazarus. (Luke 16:22-26) Jesus said that when Lazarus died, he was carried by the angels to a place called **Abraham's bosom.** However, the rich man also died, and he **was buried, and in hell he lifted up his eyes being in torments.** Lazarus and the rich man could see one another. One place was a place of comfort while the other was a place torment. The rich man could speak to Abraham, and Abraham could speak to him (vs. 24-25). These two places were in close proximity to each other, the only thing that separated the two was a great impassable gulf (vs.26). The word hell in verse 26 is the Greek word *"hades."* The Hebrew equivalent is *"sheol."* Both of these words refer to the realm of the dead.

Saved people in the Old Testament went to *Sheol.* **And all his sons and all his daughters rose up to comfort him; but he refused to be comforted; and he said, For I will go down into the grave unto my son mourning. Thus his father wept for him. (Genesis 37:35)** The word translated **grave** in this verse is the word *sheol,* it is sometimes translated hell in the Old Testament. Jacob, who was a saved man, knew that when he died he would go to sheol. The prophet Jonah prayed from this very place. **And said, I cried by reason of mine affliction unto the LORD, and he heard me; out of the belly of hell cried I, and thou heardest my voice. (Jonah 2:2)** Certainly Jonah was a saved man, but he was praying from sheol, the realm of the dead.

Sheol was made up of two parts. There was **Abraham's bosom,** where the saved went as we see in Lazarus's case. Then there was the **Hell** side where lost people like the rich man went. After Jesus paid the price for sin by dying on the cross, the saved people in Paradise were given access directly into Heaven. They could now be in the very presence of God.

Many ask, "Why couldn't they just go to Heaven when they died since they were saved?" The reason is because the price of their redemption had not been paid. It had been promised and they, by faith, believed God and were saved. **Even as Abraham believed God, and it was accounted to him for righteousness. (Galatians 3:6)** People in the Old Testament were saved by believing in the coming Messiah. But until the Messiah came and paid the price of redemption, there could be no entrance into Heaven. No one can stand in the presence of God without his sin being paid for first. This leading of the captivity had to have taken place sometime after the resurrection. At the point when Mary discovered Jesus in the garden He had not yet ascended to Heaven. **Jesus saith unto her, Touch me not; for I am not yet ascended to my Father: but go to my brethren, and say unto them, I ascend unto my Father, and your Father; and to my God, and your God. (John 20:17)** It was some time after the resurrection that Jesus descended into the lower parts of the earth and made the glorious announcement that the sin debt had been paid—the Saviour is victorious.

Peter spoke of this event as Christ preaching to those in prison. **For Christ also hath once suffered for sins, the just for the unjust, that he might bring us to God, being put to death in the flesh, but quickened by the Spirit: By which also he went and preached unto the spirits in prison. (1 Peter 3:18-19)** What a time of shouting that must have been when He gathered the saved out of the paradise side of Sheol and like the mighty victorious king who had just defeated the enemy and liberated his captives, led them into the presence of God.

THE GIFTS

And he gave some, apostles; and some, prophets; and some, evangelists; and some, pastors and teachers. (Ephesians 4:11) There are many other gifts, but there are four specific gifts listed here. These are foundational gifts given to men by God for the building of the local Church.

The Apostle

The word **apostle** comes from the Greek *"apostolos"* and means *"to send out or sent one."* In order that a man may qualify to be an apostle of Christ he had to:

1) Be personally commissioned and sent out by Christ. Paul became an apostle on the Damascus road. (Acts 9) **Paul, an apostle, (not of men, neither by man, but by Jesus Christ, and God the Father, who raised him from the dead;) ... For I neither received it of man, neither was I taught it, but by the revelation of Jesus Christ. (Galatians 1:1, 12)**

2) He had to personally see the resurrected Saviour. **Am I not an apostle? am I not free? have I not seen Jesus Christ our Lord? are not ye my work in the Lord? If I be not an apostle unto others, yet doubtless I am to you: for the seal of mine apostleship are ye in the Lord. (1 Corinthians 9:1-2)** Personally seeing the resurrected Christ was a distinguishing qualification.

The gift of Apostleship was especially designed to establish the validity of Christ's resurrection. An apostle was one who could testify, *"I have seen the resurrected Saviour, and I have this message from Him."* God endowed these apostles with special powers to perform miracles to establish their authority (Hebrews 2:1-4) as they laid the foundation of the Church. (Ephesians 2:20) When the apostles died, the position of apostle died with them. There are no apostles today.

The Prophets

Next there are **prophets.** In the Old Testament the gift of prophecy was the gift to proclaim and explain the will of God and often involved predicting future events. At the time the Church was instituted, the Word of God was not yet complete. Until completion of the written revelation, one of God's instruments to reveal His will to man was the prophet. However, since the canon of Scripture is complete, there is no need for the Prophet. Once the Word of God was completed, the gift of prophecy ceased. Paul said, **whether there be prophecies, they shall fail. (1 Corinthians 13:8)** Prophecy was a temporal sign gift. Paul told the Corinthians that it would **fail.** The word **fail** comes from the word *"kataargeo"* and means *"to be entirely idle useless, cease, become of no effect, come to naught, vanish away, make void."* From where Paul was standing in time, there would be a day in the future when the temporal gifts would come to naught. In fact, God closes the book of Revelation with this stern warning to those who claim to be Prophets.

> **For I testify unto every man that heareth the words of the prophecy of this book, If any man shall add unto these things, God shall add unto him the plagues that are written in this book: And if any man shall take away from the words of the book of this prophecy, God shall take away his part out of the book of life, and out of the holy city, and from the things which are written in this book. (Revelation 22:18-19)**

God is saying, *"My Word is complete and it is perfect. Leave it alone. There is nothing to be added or deleted."* He pronounced judgment upon the wannabe Prophets who would add to it or take away from it.

The Evangelist

The word **evangelist** comes from *"euangelistes"* and means *"a preacher of the gospel."* An evangelist is one who is called and gifted to proclaim the good news of the Gospel. (Acts 8:26-40; 21:28) He too, is a gift to the Church and should be a major part of establishing and planting churches. This gift still exists today and will continue to exist throughout the Church Age.

The Pastor

Next are **Pastors and teachers**. The term **pastors and teachers** as used here refers to the same person—the pastor-teacher is one office. There is a separate office of teacher listed in 1 Corinthians 12:28 apart from the pastor. You can be a teacher without being a pastor, but you cannot be a pastor without being a teacher. Pastor is the title. Teacher is part of the function. Paul said that the Pastor is to be **apt to teach. (1 Timothy 3:2)** The Pastor must spiritually feed the people whom God has given him. Matthew Henry comments:

> "[He is] one who is both able and willing to communicate to others the knowledge which God has given him, one who is fit to teach and ready to take all opportunities of giving instruction, who is himself well instructed in the things of the kingdom of heaven, and is communicative of what he knows to others."

The gift of teaching is the supernatural ability to explain clearly and make application of the Word of God. The Pastor's exhortation is to **Feed the flock of God which is among you... (1 Peter 5:2).** A Pastor must be faithful in preaching and teaching the Word of God. The **call** is to preach and the **content** is the Word of God.

THE GAIN

Every child of God has at least one spiritual gift and some have more than one gift. These gifts are given for the benefit of the Church. **But the manifestation of the Spirit is given to every man to profit withal. (1 Corinthians 12:7)** The Church was not designed to hobble and gimp its way through the world deprived of power and ability. God has given His people gifts so that the Church might operate at peak efficiency and reach its full potential. Now Paul talks about the gain or the benefits of the gifts. When God's people are in their place and active with their spiritual gifts, it makes a difference.

To Equip The Saints

For the perfecting of the saints.... (Ephesians 4:12a) The word translated **perfecting** comes from the Greek *"katartismos"* and means *"to make fully ready."* It carries the idea completion. The verb form of this word is found several times in Scripture. It is used of mending broken nets. (Matthew 4:21; Mark 1:19) It is used of restoring wayward brethren. (Galatians 6:1) It is a word that speaks of mending or making up for that which is lacking. These gifts are given to the Church for the purpose of mending people's lives; to impart that which is lacking in the faith and knowledge of

Christians. God gives these gifts so that we can help one another be what God expects us to be.

To Engage The Saints

As the child of God is equipped, he is to be engaged **for the work of the ministry. (Ephesians 4:12b)** Notice that the **work of the ministry** is not given to the pastor exclusively, but to every Christian. Every child of God needs to be involved in the ministry somewhere. The ministry gifts are to perfect the saints so that they can do the work of the ministry. This is where discipleship comes in. Jesus said:

> **Go ye therefore, and teach all nations, baptizing them in the name of the Father, and of the Son, and of the Holy Ghost: Teaching them to observe all things whatsoever I have commanded you: and, lo, I am with you alway, even unto the end of the world. Amen. (Matthew 28:19-20)**

Notice that there is the initial teaching about Christ—that is soul-winning. After that we are to get them into Church and down the aisle for baptism. However, take note of the next command. Jesus said, **Teaching them to observe all things whatsoever I have commanded you.** That is discipleship. That is the training and preparing of the new convert so that he can be engaged in the work of the ministry. **And the things that thou hast heard of me among many witnesses, the same commit thou to faithful men, who shall be able to teach others also. (2 Timothy 2:2)**

To Edify The Saints

The work of the ministry is **the edifying of the body of Christ: Till we all come in the unity of the faith, and of the**

knowledge of the Son of God, unto a perfect man, unto the measure of the stature of the fulness of Christ. (Ephesians 4:12c-13) The word **edifying** comes from *"oikodome"* and means to *"build up."* The word **perfect (vs. 13)** is from *"teleios"* and means *"to be mature and fully developed."* It describes the growth and development of a child into adulthood. Paul says, **Till we all come in the unity of the faith.** Notice how the unity of the faith and the maturity of the saint go together. As Christians mature and develop, unity becomes a reality.

To Establish The Saints

That we henceforth be no more children, tossed to and fro, and carried about with every wind of doctrine, by the sleight of men, and cunning craftiness, whereby they lie in wait to deceive. (Ephesians 4:14) The lack of edification results in the defeat of believers. God's desire for believers is that we **be no more children...** Many are spiritual infants when they should be mature adults in the Lord. There is nothing wrong with being a baby if you are a baby.

> **Wherefore laying aside all malice, and all guile, and hypocrisies, and envies, and all evil speakings, As newborn babes, desire the sincere milk of the word, that ye may grow thereby: (1 Peter 2:1-2)**

However if a fellow is thirty years old and is still in diapers and on milk there is something wrong. Sadly there are many Christians who are just that way. The Hebrew believers were toddlers when they should have been teachers.

> **Of whom we have many things to say, and hard to be uttered, seeing ye are dull of hearing. For**

when for the time ye ought to be teachers, ye have need that one teach you again which *be* the first principles of the oracles of God; and are become such as have need of milk, and not of strong meat. (Hebrews 5:11-12)

As one grows from infancy into an adult there are some things that must be laid aside. Paul wrote, **When I was a child, I spake as a child, I understood as a child, I thought as a child: but when I became a man, I put away childish things. (1 Corinthians 13:11)** God wants His children to grow up.

Notice the terms Paul uses in describing the saint who doesn't grow up. The term **tossed to and fro** is a nautical expression describing the agitation and tossing of waves. Not only is the immature believer tossed to and fro, but he is also **carried about with every wind of doctrine.** The expression **carried about** describes a ship that is driven around in circles by the fierce winds of a storm. The baby believer is not stable. He is constantly driven about and tossed around by every doctrine that comes down the pike. Paul goes on to describe false teachers who prey on those who fail to mature. He describes their work as **the sleight of men, and cunning craftiness, whereby they lie in wait to deceive. (Ephesians 4:14b)** The word **sleight** is from the Greek *"kybeia."* It is a gambling term and speaks of trickery and fraud. The word **craftiness** is used in the Bible to describe the way the Pharisees dealt with Jesus. It is also used of the serpents deceiving of Eve. These words speak of deceivers who speak cunningly and shrewdly. They sound correct and they are convincing, but they are wrong and dangerous. The Word of God produces stability in the believer's life. The purpose of establishing the saints is that they **be no more children, tossed to and fro.**

To Enhance The Saints

But speaking the truth in love... (Ephesians 4:15a) Maturity will sweeten the saint. There is a right way to stand. It is **speaking the truth in love...** A mature Christian will maintain a good balance of truth and love. Jesus said, **...thy word is truth. (John 17:17)** Speaking the truth is important, but speaking it in love is just as important. When a believer grows in the Word it is manifested in two ways—words and works. Both are important. Paul said, **And whatsoever ye do in word or deed, do all in the name of the Lord Jesus, giving thanks to God and the Father by him. (Colossians 3:17)** There are those today who teach that we need to forget doctrine and focus on love. By the same token, there are those who seem to know nothing of love, but they sure can blast folks with the truth. There must be balance. I hear people say, *"I'm looking for a Church where there is love."* Yet others say, *"I want a Church that stands for the truth."* The fact is, love and truth stand together. In 1Corinthians 13, Paul, by inspiration of the Holy Spirit, penned the great love chapter of the Bible. He clearly said that love, **Rejoiceth not in iniquity, but rejoiceth in the truth. (1 Corinthians 13:6)** The mature believer will be balanced in love and truth.

To Encompass The Saints

Christ's design is that we **may grow up into him in all things, which is the head, even Christ: (Ephesians 4:15b)** As we grow up into Him, we become stronger and more productive in the work of the ministry. It is from Christ, who is the head, that the body derives its direction. As a body, we function properly only as we are led by the head.

From whom the whole body fitly joined together and compacted by that which every joint supplieth, according to the effectual working in the measure of every part, maketh increase of the body unto the edifying of itself in love. (Ephesians 4:16) The words **fitly joined together** speak of a joint in the construction of a building. It speaks of two or more pieces of wood being fitted and joined perfectly for a particular place. The word **compacted** was used of reconciling two people who were at odds with one another. Both terms speak of bringing things together. Paul describes it as the **effectual working in the measure of every part.** Even a door frame properly joined and fitted together allows the door to open and close right, so every child of God, as he grows, is fitted into the local body for the **effectual working** of that local body.

The New Life In Christ
Ephesians 4:17-24

This passage of Ephesians is one the strongest appeals to Christians found in the New Testament. Here Paul calls for a complete separation from the old life. When a person becomes a Christian, he becomes a new creature with a new course.

THE COURSE OF THE SINNER

This I say therefore, and testify in the Lord, that ye henceforth walk not as other Gentiles walk, in the vanity of their mind. (Ephesians 4:17) At the moment of salvation, we are to renounce the old life. We turned from what we were to Jesus Christ for salvation. Paul warns those who are saved that they are not to walk as they did before salvation. They are not to live as they did when they were lost. Paul points out some of the character traits of the lost.

Their Mind Is Vain

Paul spoke of the condition of the lost when he said they walk **in the vanity of their mind. (Ephesians 4:17a)** The word **vanity** comes from *"mataiotes"* and means *"moral depravity."* The idea here is that God and His ways are not in their thoughts. The unsaved man's mind is empty and senseless concerning the things of God. This is by their own choice. **And even as they did not like to retain God in their knowledge, God gave them over to a reprobate mind. (Romans 1:28)** Some people have rejected God and His ways to the point that they have crossed the deadline—there is no hope for them.

Paul continues to describe them as, **Having the understanding darkened, being alienated from the life of God through the ignorance that is in them, because of the blindness of their heart. (Ephesians 4:18)** Paul mentions four reasons for the unsaved mind being in the condition that it is:

First, their **understanding** is faulty—it has been darkened! The word **understanding** means *"to exercise the mind, to grasp, comprehend, to perceive."* The basic idea is discernment. The natural man has no comprehension of spiritual things.

Second, their understanding has been **darkened.** The word **darkened** carries the idea of being *"blind and unable to see."* **In whom the god of this world hath blinded the minds of them which believe not, lest the light of the glorious gospel of Christ, who is the image of God, should shine unto them. (2 Corinthians 4:4)**

Third, they are **alienated from the life of God through the ignorance that is in them.** The word **alienated** means *"to be cut off, separated, estranged, detached."* It carries the idea of being a foreigner or an outsider.

Fourth, is the **blindness of their heart.** The word **blindness** is an interesting word. It comes from the Greek *"porosis"* and carries the idea of *"stupidity, callousness, blindness, hardness."* The things of God are obscure and incomprehensible to the lost. **But the natural man receiveth not the things of the Spirit of God: for they are foolishness unto him: neither can he know them.... (1 Corinthians**

2:14a) The natural man is the person who has not been regenerated by God. He is exactly as he was when he was born—a natural unsaved man. He lacks spiritual understanding. The things of God are **foolishness unto him: neither can he know them.**

Their Morality Is Corrupt

Who being past feeling have given themselves over unto lasciviousness, to work all uncleanness with greediness. (Ephesians 4:19) Corrupt thinking produces corrupt living. When men refuse God and push Him out of their minds, their minds are void and empty of God and of His truth and it shows up in their lifestyle. Paul says here that they have given themselves over to **lasciviousness.** The word **lasciviousness** speaks of *"unrestrained indecent and shameless behavior."* It carries the idea of having a *"license to live without restraint or as one desires."* It is living according to lustful desires. It speaks of the day in which we live. It seems that many today have no shame about their sin. There was once a time when folks would try to hide their sin. Now they flaunt it in open defiance of God's law. **Uncleanness** speaks of that which is impure or filthy and describes their lifestyles. Paul adds **greediness** to the list. Greediness comes from *"pleonexia"* and means *"fraudulency, extortion, covetous."* The idea is that of an unquenchable lust for whatever one desires. Such are the characteristics of those who know not God.

THE CHARACTER OF THE SAVIOUR

But ye have not so learned Christ; If so be that ye have heard him, and have been taught by him, as the truth is in Jesus. (Ephesians 4:20-21) These are precious words, **but**

ye. Here we turn from our past hopeless condition to what we are in Christ. We are moved from depravity to delight. As a child of God we are no longer hopelessly lost and in slavery to sin.

Paul says, **ye have not so learned Christ... (Ephesians 4:20a)** In other words, *"you didn't learn a wicked lifestyle from Christ."* This is a reference to our salvation and discipleship in Christ. Paul is clearly teaching here that we do not get saved and continue to live the same old lifestyle. To learn Christ involves far more than just salvation. Jesus said,

> **Come unto me, all ye that labour and are heavy laden, and I will give you rest. Take my yoke upon you, and learn of me; for I am meek and lowly in heart: and ye shall find rest unto your souls. For my yoke is easy, and my burden is light. (Matthew 11:28-29)**

Notice four key ingredients to the Christian life.

1) *Salvation.* **Come unto me, all ye that labour and are heavy laden, and I will give you rest.** The rest that this world longs for comes only from a personal relationship with Christ.

2) *Service.* **Take my yoke upon you.** Easy believism has offered a religion without righteousness. As a result, untold thousands have repeated a prayer but continue on without serving Christ. Such a salvation is foreign to Scripture.

3) *Schooling*. Jesus said, **learn of me.** Our first and continuing priority as a Christian is to learn all we can about our Saviour and His ways.

4) **_Satisfaction_**. Then comes the promise, **ye shall find rest unto your souls.** Satisfaction! That is what the world is looking for. Yet, they grope hopelessly in the dark failing to come to Christ where real satisfaction is found.

What a contrast that Paul gives between the old life and the new. What a difference! Salvation means a change. Paul said, **Therefore if any man be in Christ, he is a new creature: old things are passed away; behold, all things are become new. (2 Corinthians 5:17)** Notice that Paul says, **All things are become new.** True conversion results in a change of lifestyle. If you are saved, you are different from what you were.

THE CHALLENGE TO THE SAINT

That ye put off concerning the former conversation the old man, which is corrupt according to the deceitful lusts; And be renewed in the spirit of your mind; And that ye put on the new man, which after God is created in righteousness and true holiness. (Ephesians 4:22-24) We are challenged to walk according to what we are rather than what we were. Here we see the sharp contrast between the Spirit-led life and the flesh-led life. The challenge is three-fold.

There Is Something To Put Off

That ye put off concerning the former conversation the old man, which is corrupt according to the deceitful lusts. (Ephesians 4:22) The phrase **old man** is speaking of the old depraved nature that man is born into the world with. This old nature is referred to as the natural man. Paul wrote, **But**

the natural man receiveth not the things of the Spirit of God: for they are foolishness unto him: neither can he know them, because they are spiritually discerned. (1 Corinthians 2:14) It is a nature of depravity and corruption and delights in sin and wickedness. The old nature is not in subjection to the law of God. **Because the carnal mind is enmity against God: for it is not subject to the law of God, neither indeed can be. (Romans 8:7)** It is a nature that is an enemy of God and hates everything that is holy and decent. **For I know that in me (that is, in my flesh,) dwelleth no good thing: for to will is present with me; but how to perform that which is good I find not. (Romans 7:18)** It was the old depraved nature that Jeremiah was speaking of when he said, **The heart is deceitful above all things, and desperately wicked: who can know it?. (Jeremiah 17:9)** The old nature was not altered or changed at salvation, neither can it be reformed. The Bible tells us that the only method for dealing with the old nature is crucifixion. Paul said, **I am crucified with Christ: nevertheless I live; yet not I, but Christ liveth in me: and the life which I now live in the flesh I live by the faith of the Son of God, who loved me, and gave himself for me. (Galatians 2:20)** Again, to the Romans, Paul wrote, **For if ye live after the flesh, ye shall die: but if ye through the Spirit do mortify the deeds of the body, ye shall live. (Romans 8:13)** The old nature must be put off. It can be crucified and controlled, but it cannot be tamed or reformed.

There Is Something To Put In

And be renewed in the spirit of your mind. (Ephesians 4:23) We are commanded to put off the old and put on the new. This is the difference between defeat and victory. If we live in the flesh we will be a defeated believer. However, if we put off the flesh and put on the new, we can be a victorious believer. What must be understood here is that the mind is the battleground between the old and the new. The word **renewed** is the same as used in Romans where Paul commanded, **be not conformed to this world: but be ye transformed by the renewing of your mind, that ye may prove what is that good, and acceptable, and perfect, will of God. (Romans 12:2)** Renewing comes from *"anakainosis"* and means to *"renovate, reform, refurbish, and correct."* Our thinking determines our direction. The Bible clearly teaches that a man is, in practice, what he is in his heart. Solomon warned us, **Keep thy heart with all diligence; for out of it are the issues of life. (Proverbs 4:23)** If we are going to be right we are going to have to think right!

There Is Something To Put On

And that ye put on the new man, which after God is created in righteousness and true holiness. (Ephesians 4:24) By the phrase **new man** Paul is speaking of the new nature which is given to us as the result of being born again. **Therefore if any man be in Christ, he is a new creature: old things are passed away; behold, all things are become new. (2 Corinthians 5:17)** Jesus said, **That which is born of the Spirit is spirit. (John 3:6)** This is the new birth when one becomes a **partaker of the divine nature. (2 Peter 1:4)** The new nature cannot and will not sin because it is born of God. **Whosoever is born of God doth not commit sin; for his seed remaineth in him: and he cannot sin, because he is born of God. (1 John 3:9)** When the believer sins it is because he submits and succumbs to the old nature. If he lives for God it is because he is submitted to and living in the Spirit.

These two natures abide side by side in the child of God until the redemption of the body. That will take place when the Lord Jesus Christ appears in the rapture to take His people out of this world. **Beloved, now are we the sons of God, and it doth not yet appear what we shall be: but we know that, when he shall appear, we shall be like him; for we shall see him as he is. (1 John 3:2)** What a day that will be—the rapture and glorification of the saints. But, look what else! John declares, **we shall be like Him. (1 John 3:2)** Sin will be forever banished from the Christian's life. But until then we must put off, put in, and put on.

The New You
Ephesians 4:25-32

Duty always follows doctrine. Paul has just instructed the believer to put off the old man and put on the new. He now makes application.

STOP LYING

Wherefore putting away lying, speak every man truth with his neighbour: for we are members one of another. (Ephesians 4:25) The word **lying** simply means to speak falsely. It is a deception, misrepresentation, or exaggeration. Lying can show up in several forms. It can be an outright lie or it can be what some excuse as a *"little white lie."* A lie is a lie regardless of how it is dressed up. Leon Morris said, *"Lying may be an accepted weapon in the warfare waged by the worldly, but it has no place in the life of the Christian."* God takes lying seriously. He said, **... all liars, shall have their part in the lake which burneth with fire and brimstone: which is the second death. (Revelation 21:8)**

We are not to lie, but speak truth one to another because, **we are members one of another.** We are a family, a family that is built upon truth. You can't have unity, true love, and peace in a family where there is a liar. Since God's family must be built upon truth, lying puts the family in danger. John Chrysostom said, *"If the eye sees a serpent, does it deceive the foot? If the tongue tastes what is bitter, does it deceive the stomach?"* John Mackay said, *"A lie is a stab into the very vitals of the Body of Christ."* We expect lying from the lost world. They picked it up from their father, the

Devil. Jesus said to a bunch of liars, **Ye are of your father the devil, and the lusts of your father ye will do. He was a murderer from the beginning, and abode not in the truth, because there is no truth in him. When he speaketh a lie, he speaketh of his own: for he is a liar, and the father of it. (John 8:44)** God's people must be truthful. There is absolutely no place or excuse for lying among believers.

SHORTEN ANGER

Be ye angry, and sin not: let not the sun go down upon your wrath. (Ephesians 4:26) Anger is a dangerous enemy. Here we are told that it is possible to be **angry, and sin not.** This kind of anger is called righteous indignation. Indignation describes anger that is the result of an injustice or sin committed against someone. It is most of the time a righteous anger. Noah Webster defines indignation as

> "Anger or extreme anger, mingled with contempt, disgust or abhorrence ... The anger of a superior; extreme anger; particularly, the wrath of God against sinful men for their ingratitude and rebellion ... The effects of anger; the dreadful effects of God's wrath; terrible judgments ... Holy displeasure at one's self for sin."

Indignation is a righteous anger that is free from rage and retaliation. It is a wholesome anger aimed at the problem and not the person. Even though our anger may be righteous, we are still admonished **let not the sun go down upon your wrath.** When we are angered about something, we must deal with it. We cannot end the day and go to bed with our anger eating at us. David said it this way, **Cease from anger, and forsake wrath: fret not thyself in any wise** to do evil. (Psalm 37:8) **C**ease simply means to *"stop or to abstain."* Don't sit around and wait for your offender to apologize.

SHUN THE DEVIL

Neither give place to the devil. (Ephesians 4:27) The word **place** carries the idea of *"opportunity."* When we fail to put off the old and put on the new we give Satan an opportunity to gain ground in our life. We can be certain that he will take advantage of every opportunity that we give him.

START WORKING

Let him that stole steal no more: but rather let him labour, working with his hands the thing which is good, that he may have to give to him that needeth. (Ephesians 4:28) The word **steal** means *"to cheat or to take something wrongfully from another."* As Christians we are not takers, instead we are to work so we will have something to give to those who are in need. Giving and caring for others is a trait of God's family. **But whoso hath this world's good, and seeth his brother have need, and shutteth up his bowels of compassion from him, how dwelleth the love of God in him? (1 John 3:17)** Christians are givers, not takers. So much for the welfare mentality that is so prevalent today.

SPEAK RIGHT

Let no corrupt communication proceed out of your mouth, but that which is good to the use of edifying, that it may minister grace unto the hearers. (Ephesians 4:29) The word **corrupt** means *"rotten or foul."* It carries the idea of being putrid and was used in Paul's day to describe spoiled food. This speaks of passing on rumors, slander, bad and off color jokes, and any talk that is not wholesome. Paul contrasts **corrupt communication** to **that which is good to the use of edifying, that it may minister grace unto the hearers.** We are to speak good and wholesome words that minister rather than rotten and putrid words that hurt. We are to use our tongues to Enlighten, Evangelize, Establish, Exhort, Encourage, and Edify others. Like David we must bridle our tongue. **...I said, I will take heed to my ways, that I sin not with my tongue: I will keep my mouth with a bridle, while the wicked is before me. (Psalms 39:1)**

SATISFY THE SPIRIT

And grieve not the holy Spirit of God, whereby ye are sealed unto the day of redemption. (Ephesians 4:30) The word **grieve** means *"to give pain of mind to; to afflict; to wound the feelings."* Keep in mind that the Holy Spirit who dwells in each believer is God and therefore He is grieved by our sin. We should never allow anything in our affections, thoughts, words, or deeds which would grieve our indwelling Comforter. Our sin inflicts great pain upon God.

SWEETEN UP

Let all bitterness, and wrath, and anger, and clamour, and evil speaking, be put away from you, with all malice. (Ephesians 4:31) Paul lists six more sins that need to be dealt with in order to sweeten our life.

First, put away **Bitterness. (Ephesians 4:31a)** Bitterness is a deep seated, long burning and smoldering resentment. It is an anger that is constantly brooding and holding grudges. Noah Webster says that bitterness is *"an extreme enmity, grudge, hatred; or rather an excessive degree or* *implacableness of passions and emotions."* Paul describes bitterness as the state of those who have failed of the grace of God and therefore are troubled and defiled. **Looking diligently lest any man fail of the grace of God; lest any root of bitterness springing up trouble you, and thereby many be defiled. (Hebrews 12:15)** Bitterness is always self-inflicted. Bitterness is not something that someone can do to you. Only we can do it to ourselves. Bitterness is anger in its most poisonous stage. It is a deep seated anger that has stewed deep down inside until it's poison now rules the heart. It is the most dangerous form of anger. Someone said, *"resentment is like taking poison and waiting for the other person to die."* Bitterness is destructive and deadly.

Second, put away **wrath. (Ephesians 4:31b)** Wrath carries the idea of swelling with anger. It is a boiling anger. Earl White said, *"It derives from a desire of the flesh to strike out at anything that threatens self-interests. It is a desire to take vengeance out of the hands of God and take it to ourselves."* Wrath is an anger that holds grudges. It is a get even, retaliatory anger. The wrathful person is not satisfied until he sees his offender hurt. It is an **eye for an eye, and a tooth for a tooth** philosophy. The Bible has many warnings against this kind of anger. **Wherefore, my beloved brethren, let every man be swift to hear, slow to speak, slow to wrath: for the wrath of man worketh not the righteousness of God. (James 1:19-20)**

Third, put away **Anger. (Ephesians 4:31c)** Anger is the first stage of all these other accompanying sins. According to Webster the word anger comes from a word that means to choke, strangle, or vex. He further defines anger as *"A violent passion of the mind excited by a real or supposed injury; usually accompanied with a propensity to take* vengeance, or to obtain satisfaction from the offending party.* "The Baker Encyclopedia of Psychology defines anger as *an emotional readiness to aggress.* Such people are often called *Hot Heads.* Solomon said, **A fool's wrath is presently known... (Proverbs 12:16)** One thing is for certain! Anger is not a pretty thing.

Fourth, put away **clamour. (Ephesians 4:31d)** Webster defines clamour as *"a great outcry; exclamation; made by a loud human voice continued or repeated ... It often expresses complaint and urgent demand."* **Clamour** speaks of the loud self-assertion of the angry man who is set on making sure that everyone else hears his grievance. An angry person can certainly make a lot of noise.

Fifth, put away **evil speaking. (Ephesians 4:31e)** This is slander, backbiting, angry expressions, tale-bearing and such sins of the tongue. Dr. John R. Rice said, *"More people sin with the tongue than any other way."* James had a great deal to say about the tongue. **If any man among you seem to be religious, and bridleth not his tongue, but deceiveth his own heart, this man's religion is vain. (James 1:26)** If a man claims to be a mature Christian but can't keep his own tongue from corrupt communication, he has already identified himself as deceived and his religion as vain. James went on to say, **And the tongue is a fire, a world of iniquity: so is the tongue among our members, that it defileth the whole body, and setteth on fire the course of nature; and it is set on fire of hell. (James 3:6)** A loose and smoldering tongue is not lit with any ordinary fire, it is **set on fire of hell.** The work of the uncontrolled tongue is a product of hell. A man who cannot control his tongue is doing the Devil's work. **An hypocrite with his mouth destroyeth his neighbour... (Proverbs 11:9)** Contentious,

Critical, Careless, and Corrupt communication is the work of a wicked tongue. Like the poison of a viper, the tongue is armed with the lethal venom of hate, hostility, and destructive words of death. **Their throat is an open sepulchre; with their tongues they have used deceit; the poison of asps is under their lips: Whose mouth is full of cursing and bitterness. (Romans 3:13-14)** There have been many problems and heartaches caused by angry and bitter Christians who have turned the reigns of their tongues over to hell.

Sixth, put away **malice. (Ephesians 4:31f)** Webster defines **malice** as *"Extreme enmity of heart, or malevolence; a disposition to injure others without cause, from mere personal gratification or from a spirit of revenge; unprovoked malignity or spite."* Malice is a driving desire and determination to destroy someone. There is no place for malice in the believer's life.

SPARE OTHERS

And be ye kind one to another, tenderhearted, forgiving one another, even as God for Christ's sake hath forgiven you. (Ephesians 4:32) This verse not only commands us to forgive, it tells us how to forgive. *First,* Paul says, **be ye kind.** The word **kind** means to be *"disposed to do good to others, and to make them happy by granting their requests, supplying their wants or assisting them in distress; having tenderness or goodness of nature; benevolent."* It carries the idea of being gentle, caring, courteous, good, and giving. It is the exact opposite of what anger makes us want to do. Being kind one to another is a command many times repeated in the word of God (Romans 12:10, Colossians 3:12).

Second, we are commanded to be **tenderhearted.** Webster says that the word tender speaks of *"one that attends or takes care of another."* It describes a nurse caring for a patient. Now we're not only commanded to be kind to the fellow that wronged us, we are commanded to serve him. Being **tenderhearted** means that we show compassion, mercy, sympathy, love, and tenderness, toward others. It means that we are aware of their difficulties and problems and we exercise mercy in our dealings with them (Matthew 5:7, Luke 6:36, John 13:35).

Third, we are to **forgiving**. Once we are **kind** and **tenderhearted** we can be actively **forgiving one another, even as God for Christ's sake hath forgiven you.** Notice that **forgiving** is in the present tense. Forgiving others is something that we will have to do over and over. We are reminded of the Divine standard for forgiveness! Paul points out, **As God for Christ's sake hath forgiven you.** We don't wait until restitution is made. We forgive because we have been forgiven. We do not hold out for an apology. We simply forgive. Well, you say, "I was wronged." Yes! So was God and He forgave us. We forgive because we are forgiven. We simply follow God's example. **Who is a God like unto thee, that pardoneth iniquity, and passeth by the transgression of the remnant of his heritage? he retaineth not his anger for ever, because he delighteth in mercy. (Micah 7:18)** God, forgiving our sin and giving us His best is the basis for us forgiving one another.

Imitating God
Ephesians 5:1-7

We often hear the phrase *"Like father, like son."* There is a lot of truth in that statement. Children do take after their parents. Like children who like to imitate what they see their parents do, we ought to have a desire to be like our heavenly Father.

THE PLEA

Be ye therefore followers of God, as dear children. (Ephesians 5:1) The word **followers** comes from the Greek *"mimetes"* and means *"to imitate."* The idea is that of a child imitating his parents. So too should the children of God imitate their heavenly Father. The Christian is born of God. John wrote, **Whosoever is born of God doth not commit sin; for his seed remaineth in him: and he cannot sin, because he is born of God. (1 John 3:9)** The word **seed** comes from Greek *"sperma."* Sperm is the carrier of the genes, which passes on heredity. The seed speaks of the Divine nature of God which resides in the believer. Peter spoke of believers as being **...partakers of the divine nature, having escaped the corruption that is in the world through lust. (2 Peter 1:4)** God's children do not habitually practice sin because they are born of God. The Christian possesses the nature of God and sin is contrary to His nature. Christ came to destroy the works of the devil and those born of God have His seed in them. Christ, if He lives in us and controls us, will not produce unrighteousness. Because we are born of God and have the nature of God in us, we are to exhibit the traits of God. In the context of (Ephesians 4:32-5:2) we are to imitate our Heavenly Father.

THE PATH

And walk in love... (Ephesians 5:2a) The plea is to be like God. Our path is to walk as He walks. The word walk speaks of lifestyle. One of the great traits of a Christian ought to be love. The doctrine of love is a foundational truth. The Bible is full of exhortations to love. **Beloved, let us love one another: for love is of God; and every one that loveth is born of God, and knoweth God. He that loveth not knoweth not God; for God is love. (1 John 4:7-8)** True love originates in God, **for love is of God.** The Christian's love flows from God. **The love of God is shed abroad in our hearts by the Holy Ghost which is given unto us. (Romans 5:5)**

He that loveth not knoweth not God; for God is love. (1 John 4:8) One who claims to be a Christian, but does not manifest God's love in his life, is like the person who claims to have been born of parents he does not in any way resemble. This verse is simple to understand. If we truly know Christ as Saviour, because He is love, we will love.

THE PATTERN

... as Christ also hath loved us, and hath given himself for us an offering and a sacrifice to God for a sweetsmelling savour. (Ephesians 5:2b) The pattern for Christian living is Christ Himself. We just read in the previous chapter, **And be ye kind one to another, tenderhearted, forgiving one another, even as God for Christ's sake hath forgiven you. (Ephesians 4:32)** We are to imitate Christ in our dealings with others. On the night of the Lord's Supper Jesus revealed to the disciples that He would soon die. He then instructed His disciples:

A new commandment I give unto you, that ye love one another; as I have loved you, that ye also love one another. By this shall all men know that ye are my disciples, if ye have love one to another. (John 13:34-35)

Notice that our Lord calls this a **new** commandment. The command to love one another was not new. So far as man is concerned love is as old as the law. Moses said, **thou shalt love thy neighbour as thyself. (Leviticus 19:18)** However, Jesus' command to love was new because He gave it a new standard. Grace always carries a greater responsibility than law. No longer do we love each other as we love our self, but Jesus said to **love one another; as I have loved you.** He loved us all the way to the cross. **Greater love hath no man than this, that a man lay down his life for his friends. (John 15:13)** It is one thing to say I love you, but it is quite another to show it. God not only said I love you; He demonstrated His love for us. **But God commendeth his love toward us, in that, while we were yet sinners, Christ died for us. (Romans 5:8)** Jesus left us with the responsibility to love one another in the same manner in which He loved us–sacrificially. Jesus also said, **By this shall all men know that ye are my disciples, if ye have love one to another.** Our love for each other is evidence that we are His disciples.

THE PURITY

But fornication, and all uncleanness, or covetousness, let it not be once named among you, as becometh saints. (Ephesians 5:3) Previously Paul described true Christian love. He used Christ's sacrifice as a pattern for Biblical love. Christ's love is a love that sacrifices for the person loved. Sadly this world knows very little of such a love. The world's love is seen in the movies, soap operas and vulgar magazines. What the world calls love, God calls lust. This world has perverted love into fornication, adultery and sexual abuse of all kinds. Sex sells everything from soft drinks to cars. Most billboards, radio spots, television advertisements, and magazine ads usually contain some kind of sexual perversion. Paul hits us where we live—children of God in a sex driven society. In verses 3-7 Paul deals with sexual perversion and how to stay pure in a filthy world.

The Definition of Fornication

Paul names the sin of **fornication, and all uncleanness, or covetousness. (Ephesians 5:3a)** Webster defines **fornication** as, *"The incontinence* [no restraint, free or uncontrolled indulgence of the passions] *or lewdness of unmarried persons, male or female; also, the criminal conversation* [behavior] *of a married man with an unmarried woman."* It is the word from which we get pornography, and refers to any illicit sexual activity. Notice the words that Paul uses in connection with fornication.

Uncleanness speaks of any form of impurity. We are to be a clean people as opposed to uncleanness. We are to be a people of the Word and therefore, a clean people. Speaking of Jesus and the Church the Bible says, **That he might sanctify and cleanse it with the washing of water by the word. (Ephesians 5:26)** People who fail to stay in the Bible will live an unclean life. Jesus said, **Now ye are clean**

through the word which I have spoken unto you. (John 15:3)

Covetousness is from the word *"pleonexia"* and means *"fraudulency, extortion, covetous, ruthless greed."* The idea is that of an unquenchable lust for whatever one desires. Earlier Paul wrote, **Who being past feeling have given themselves over unto lasciviousness, to work all uncleanness with greediness. (Ephesians 4:19)** The same word translated **covetousness** in Ephesians 5:3 is translated **greediness** in (Ephesians 4:19). Greed and covetousness are the complete opposite of Christ's love. Christ's love is a sacrificing love. Fornication is selfish indulgence at the expense of others.

Paul says, **let it not be once named among you, as becometh saints. (Ephesians 5:3b)** Contrary to what the world thinks, moral absolutes do exist, and their foundation is in the Word of God. The Bible is unmistakably clear that sex is to be between husband and wife. Anything else is perversion. **Marriage is honourable in all, and the bed undefiled: but whoremongers and adulterers God will judge. (Hebrews 13:4)**

The Development of Fornication

Neither filthiness, nor foolish talking, nor jesting, which are not convenient: but rather giving of thanks. (Ephesians 5:4) Paul uses three more words to describe conduct and speech that is to have no place in the Christian's life. These words show us how an unclean lifestyle develops.

*First, **Filthy Shamelessness**.* This word **filthiness** is from the Greek *"aischrotes"* and has the basic meaning of *"obscenity and shamefulness."* It refers to that which one ought to be ashamed of, that which would make a moral person blush. **What fruit had ye then in those things whereof ye are now ashamed? for the end of those things is death. (Romans 6:21)** Have you noticed that folks don't blush much anymore. Child of God, there are certain things that ought to make you blush. Even in this wicked society where filthiness is accepted as commonplace. God help us not to become so desensitized to the filthiness of the unsaved world that it no longer bothers us.

*Second, **Foolish Speech**.* The child of God is not to be engaged in **foolish talking.** This speaks of conversation that is empty, profitless, idle, or obscene. The word foolish comes from the Greek *"aischrotes"* and carries the idea of *"buffoonery and stupidity."* It speaks of silly or foolish talk that just wastes time and profits nothing. It is talk that nothing good can come from. Dirty jokes and lighthearted talk about sexual topics fall into this category. Such talk has no place in the life of a Christian. **In the multitude of words there wanteth not sin: but he that refraineth his lips is wise. (Proverbs 10:19)**

*Third, **Flippant Silliness**.* Paul warns about **jesting**. The word jesting comes from the Greek *"eutrapelia"* and means *"witticism, ribaldry."* It is the art of being good at turning one's speech for the purpose of laughter. It is to joke, talk foolishly, poke fun, or to make wisecracks. It is taking something that someone has said or done, no matter how innocent, and turning it into that which is obscene or suggestive. Kenneth Wuest says that it also carries the idea of being cunning and clever, of being polished in suggestive and off-colored joking and using it to attract attention and win favors.

What is the alternative to such speech? Paul says that we should be occupied rather with the **giving of thanks. (Ephesians 5:4)** John Stott said,

> "All God's gifts, including sex, are subjects for thanksgiving, rather than for joking. To joke about them is bound to degrade them; to thank God for them is the way to preserve their worth as the blessings of a loving Creator."

Now Paul is not forbidding speaking about sex, nor is he forbidding all humor, but he is saying that we should not waste our time with fifthly, frivolous, and foolish talk that harms spiritual life.

The Danger of Fornication

For this ye know, that no whoremonger, nor unclean person, nor covetous man, who is an idolater, hath any inheritance in the kingdom of Christ and of God. (Ephesians 5:5) Paul issues a solemn warning to those who are caught up in such a lifestyle. Paul dogmatically stated that they have no **inheritance in the kingdom of Christ and of God.** No **whoremonger, unclean person, covetous man,** or **idolater** will have any part in Heaven. Though it is not popular in these wicked times, we must nevertheless take God at His Word. Such people will not inherit the kingdom. Of course this isn't speaking of someone who sins, but goes on to repent and gets victory over the sin. This is speaking of those who claim to be Christians, but their lives are marked by the wicked lifestyle described. Anyone can be forgiven and have victory over sin. However, those who habitually practice such a lifestyle with no conviction and no concern for the testimony of Christ are not God's children. **But it is happened unto them according to the true proverb, The dog is turned to his own vomit again; and the sow that was washed to her wallowing in the mire. (2 Peter 2:22)**

Paul warns, **Let no man deceive you with vain words: for because of these things cometh the wrath of God upon the children of disobedience. (Ephesians 5:6)** Those who believe that they can repeat a little prayer and live in sin with no change of lifestyle and then go to Heaven are deceived.

The Departure from Fornication

Be not ye therefore partakers with them. (Ephesians 5:7) This verse makes it clear that Christians must not partake of the sins of the unbelievers. Holy living doesn't just happen. It is a choice based upon obedience to the clear commands of Scripture. We must make a daily choice to walk with God, stay in His Word, and to separate from wickedness. **Be not ye therefore partakers with them.** This is a very clear command.

Living In The Light
Ephesians 5:8-14

Light is one of the metaphors used in the Word of God to describe both God and His people. The Bible declares that **God is light, and in him is no darkness at all. (1 John 1:5b)** Light expresses God's holiness, glory and presence. Jesus said, **I am the light of the world: he that followeth me shall not walk in darkness, but shall have the light of life. (John 8:12)** Jesus said, **As long as I am in the world, I am the light of the world. (John 9:5)** Here Paul stresses the truth that believers are light.

THE CONTRAST

For ye were sometimes darkness, but now are ye light in the Lord: walk as children of light. (Ephesians 5:8) Notice that Paul said we **were** (past tense) darkness, but now we **are** (present tense) light in the Lord. This is a marvelous truth. The Word of God speaks of believers being in the light and of the light, but notice here that we **are** light. We're not merely in the light and we are not just of the light, but Paul says, **now are ye light in the Lord.** Jesus said, **Ye are the light of the world. (Matthew 5:14)** It is clear that there is an absolute difference between the unsaved life and the life in Christ. We no longer belong to the realm of darkness. **Who hath delivered us from the power of darkness, and hath translated us into the kingdom of his dear Son. (Colossians 1:13)** Peter said, **But ye are a chosen generation, a royal priesthood, an holy nation, a peculiar people; that ye should show forth the praises of him who hath called you out of darkness into his marvellous light. (1 Peter 2:9)** Being His children and now having His nature we no longer belong to the realm of darkness. Notice that Paul adds the command, **walk as children of light. (Ephesians 5:8b)** In other words, we are children of God so let's live like it.

THE CHARACTERISTICS

(For the fruit of the Spirit is in all goodness and righteousness and truth;) Proving what is acceptable unto the Lord. (Ephesians 5:9-10) A life lived by the power of God's Spirit will have several characteristics in particular.

The Product Of The Spirit

Goodness is from the Greek *"agathosyne"* and speaks of goodness in the sense of *"honesty and integrity of heart."* It is goodness that not only despises evil, but refrains from doing it. It is a lifestyle that is produced by a heart condition. It is conviction with action. That which a man truly believes, he lives. **For as he thinketh in his heart, so is he. (Proverbs 23:7a)** This goodness is a characteristic of God. David said, **I had fainted, unless I had believed to see the goodness of the LORD in the land of the living. (Psalm 27:13)** This same **goodness** is reproduced in the Christian's life as he yields to the Holy Spirit. It is a quality that we need in dealing with others. **As we have therefore opportunity, let us do good unto all men, especially unto them who are of the household of faith. (Galatians 6:10)**

Next, there is **righteousness.** Noah Webster defines **righteousness** as, *"Purity of heart and rectitude of life; conformity of heart and life to the divine law... It includes all we call justice, honesty and virtue, with holy affections; in short, it is true religion."* A truly righteous life is the result of a righteous and pure heart. It is not enough to just talk about having a righteous standing with Christ. Praise God, the believer is righteous in Christ. (2 Corinthians 5:21) However, we must also live a righteous life. Jesus Christ said, **For I say unto you, That except your righteousness shall exceed the righteousness of the scribes and Pharisees, ye shall in no case enter into the kingdom of heaven. (Matthew 5:20)** To the Pharisees, righteousness was conformity to rules; it was an external thing that completely overlooked the real condition of the heart. We don't live righteously to be righteous. We live righteously because we are righteous. God is not looking for external, self-righteousness. He is looking for righteousness that comes from a pure heart. **Flee also youthful lusts: but follow righteousness, faith, charity, peace, with them that call on the Lord out of a pure heart. (2 Timothy 2:22)**

Next, Paul points out that **truth** is a product of the Holy Spirit. Truth is that which is reliable and trustworthy. The importance of absolute truth cannot be over emphasized. Jesus said, **I am the way, the truth, and the life: no man cometh unto the Father, but by me. (John 14:6)** If Jesus is the truth, then truth is extremely important. Jesus said, **And ye shall know the truth, and the truth shall make you free. (John 8:32)** Jesus is the living truth, but praise God we also have the written truth. In Christ's great High Priestly prayer He prayed for His disciples and requested of the Father that He, **Sanctify them through thy truth: thy word is truth. (John 17:17)** Without absolute truth we have nothing. Solomon said, **For my mouth shall speak truth... (Proverbs 8:7a)** May we be a people of truth.

The Proving Of The Spirit

Proving what is acceptable unto the Lord. (Ephesians 5:10) The word **proving** comes from *"dokimazo"* and *"means* *to put something to the test, to examine by scrutinizing with discernment.*" We are to examine matters in the light of God's Word and either approve or reject them according to principle, not according to feelings, not according to what is popular, not according to what others are doing, but according to God's Word. The word **acceptable** comes from *"euarestos"* and means *"fully agreeable, acceptable well-pleasing."* Our activities, attitudes, apparel, and associations are to be well pleasing to God? Notice carefully the qualifying statement **unto the Lord,** not what is acceptable to society, not what is acceptable to Oprah, but that which is acceptable to God.

THE COMMAND

And have no fellowship with the unfruitful works of darkness, but rather reprove them. (Ephesians 5:11) Biblical separation is based upon one of God's essential attributes—His holiness. **But as he which hath called you is holy, so be ye holy in all manner of conversation; Because it is written, Be ye holy; for I am holy. (1 Peter 1:15-16)** Notice the two-fold command of this verse.

We Are To Remove Ourselves From Works Of Darkness

And have no fellowship with the unfruitful works of darkness. (Ephesians 5:11a) The command is very clear! There is to be **no fellowship** with evil. We are not to ignore the evil. We are not to compromise. We are not to reach some agreement with evil. We are light and there can be no fellowship between light and darkness. Light drives out darkness. The two cannot coexist. Paul asked ... **what communion hath light with darkness? (2 Corinthians 6:14)** Our obligation as Christians is to live holy and separated lives. Paul said that God **...saved us, and called us with an**

holy calling, not according to our works, but according to his own purpose and grace, which was given us in Christ Jesus before the world began. (2 Timothy 1:9) God has a purpose for every believer. John said, **This then is the message which we have heard of him, and declare unto you, that God is light, and in him is no darkness at all. If we say that we have fellowship with him, and walk in darkness, we lie, and do not the truth. (1 John 1:5-6)** According to John, for one to say that he is a child of God, while living in habitual sin, is to prove himself a liar. Jesus said, **I am come a light into the world, that whosoever believeth on me should not abide in darkness. (John 12:46)** If you walk with the Light—you will walk in the light. **The night is far spent, the day is at hand: let us therefore cast off the works of darkness, and let us put on the armour of light. (Romans 13:12)**

We Are To Reprove The Works Of Darkness

Paul commands, **but rather reprove them. (Ephesians 5:11b)** It is not enough to separate, we must also speak out. This verse lays a great deal of responsibility on believers. We are to warn others about the **unfruitful works of darkness.** The word **reprove** comes from the Greek *"elencho"* and means *"to confute, admonish, tell a fault, rebuke."* It carries the idea of *"bringing into the light and exposing."* We are to bring these unfruitful works of darkness into the light and expose them for what they are.

THE CONTAMINATION

For it is a shame even to speak of those things which are done of them in secret. (Ephesians 5:12) Paul goes much further than mere separation. He tells us not to even talk about the works of darkness. Some things are so evil that they are not to be subjects of discussion. What unbelievers have done in the dark is best left in the dark. **But all things that are reproved are made manifest by the light: for whatsoever doth make manifest is light. (Ephesians 5:13)** Instead of speaking of these awful deeds, Christians expose them by living lives different from world. Jesus said, **Let your light so shine before men, that they may see your good works, and glorify your Father which is in heaven. (Matthew 5:16)** A godly life is the best argument against sin.

THE CALL

Wherefore he saith, Awake thou that sleepest, and arise from the dead. (Ephesians 5:14a) Paul pulls a thought out of Isaiah 60:1-2 expressing the need for God's people to wake up and get about His business. We are warned and admonished to, **Be sober, be vigilant; because your adversary the devil, as a roaring lion, walketh about, seeking whom he may devour. (1 Peter 5:8)** The word **sober** means to be "*discreet and cautious*" and carries the idea of "*discerning.*" The word **vigilant** means to "*be awake or on the lookout.*" This is no time for slumber. Satan is looking for an opportunity to move in and devour his prey. The forces of evil are at work and we need to be awake.

... and Christ shall give thee light. (Ephesians 5:14b) Though we once groped in the darkness of depravity, that is no longer the case. Paul said, **Ye are all the children of light, and the children of the day: we are not of the night, nor of darkness. (1 Thessalonians 5:4-5)** Jesus said, **I am the light of the world: he that followeth me shall not walk in darkness, but shall have the light of life. (John 8:12)**

Walking Circumspectly
Ephesians 5:15-17

Walk speaks of lifestyle. We will walk either as foolish or as wise Christians. The foolish man loves and lives for the temporal things of this world. The wise man lives for the eternal things of God. He sets his **affection on things above, not on things on the earth. (Colossians 3:2)** Here Paul calls upon believers to walk circumspectly.

A WALK THAT REQUIRES DISCIPLINE

See then that ye walk circumspectly, not as fools, but as wise. (Ephesians 5:15) In order to enjoy a wise walk we must see to it that we **walk circumspectly.** Noah Webster defines **circumspectly** as *"cautiously; with watchfulness every way; with attention to guard against surprise or danger."* It means to walk accurately and precisely. Louis Talbot says:

> "Circumspectly means to pick the way, to be careful how we walk, as though we were walking on a ground filled with broken bottles. In Australia people build high brick walls with soft cement on top around their property. Before the cement dries, broken bottles and other pieces of glass are stuck in so that when it dries sharp edges protrude, preventing an intruder from climbing over it. A cat walking on the top of such a wall carefully places her feet between the pieces of broken glass. She picks her way. She is doing what Paul says we are to do as we walk through life's pilgrimage. The devil has scattered plenty of glass in our way; he has thrown varieties of nets, traps and snares in our path in order to destroy our Christian

testimony. But we are to walk circumspectly as resurrected people."

We must walk cautiously with watchfulness to guard against any danger. Peter warned us to, **Be sober, be vigilant; because your adversary the devil, as a roaring lion, walketh about, seeking whom he may devour: (1 Peter 5:8)** This graphic picture expresses both the danger and the confidence of Satan. Just as a blood thirsty lion stalks its prey, Satan stalks the Christian. Satan is pictured here as a **roaring lion.** A lion never roars while it is stalking. No lion stalking its prey announces it by roaring. The lion roars only after he has spotted his prey and is ready to pounce. If we wait until we hear the roar it is too late.

A WALK THAT REQUIRES DEDICATION

Redeeming the time, because the days are evil. (Ephesians 5:16) Redeeming means *to purchase; to buy up; to make the most of.* It is a commercial term that speaks of making an investment for the purpose of earning a profit. When referring to time, as in our context, it means that we are to make sure that no time is lost. God has given us a certain amount of time and we have an obligation to make sure that He gets a profitable return on His investment.

A WALK THAT REQUIRES DISCERNMENT

Discernment is the need of the hour.

We are to Shun Foolishness

We are emphatically commanded, **be ye not unwise. (Ephesians 5:17a)** It carries the idea of being senseless and without direction. The word **unwise** refers to a Christian who has little or no doctrinal understanding. His direction will be wrong because he does not know God's will. He does not know God's will because he is unwise concerning the truth of God.

We are to Study Scripturally

Rather than being unwise and foolish, Paul says we are to have **understanding.** The word **understanding** is defined by Webster as, "*comprehending; apprehending the ideas or sense of another, or of a writing; learning or being informed.*" It is the Word of God that makes us wise. **For the LORD giveth wisdom: out of his mouth cometh knowledge and understanding. (Proverbs 2:6)** Wisdom doesn't come primarily from the newspaper. The latest best seller is not our source of wisdom. There are a lot of good books out there and I enjoy reading good books. However, when we allow man's books to take the place of reading God's Book we are in trouble. No other book can do for the believer what the Bible does. The Bible is:

- Our **Counselor** When I'm **Discouraged**
- Our **Companion** When I'm **Deserted**
- Our **Comfort** When I'm **Depressed**
- Our **Candle** When It's **Dark**
- Our **Compass** When I **Doubt**
- Our **Consultant** When I **Decide**

The Bible is everything to the believer. One of the reasons we have so many failing and miserable Christians today is because of their failure to obtain God's wisdom. **Happy is the man that findeth wisdom, and the man that getteth understanding. (Proverbs 3:13)** No wonder Job said, **Neither have I gone back from the commandment of his**

lips; I have esteemed the words of his mouth more than my necessary food. (Job 23:12)

We are to Serve Faithfully

Paul said, **understanding what the will of the Lord is. (Ephesians 5:17)** The Christian will never do the will of God until he understands what God's will is. Paul equates knowing the Word of God with doing the Will of God. Jesus said, **Ye do err, not knowing the scriptures.... (Matthew 22:29)** So many people have missed the will of God because they do not know the Word of God.

Someone has well said, *"To know the will of God is the greatest knowledge. To find the will of God is the greatest discovery. To do the will of God is the greatest achievement."* The great Missionary, David Livingstone said, *"I had rather be in the heart of Africa in the will of God than on the throne of England out of the will of God."* Are you serving faithfully where God wants you?

The Spirit Filled Life
Ephesians 5:18-21

A Spirit-filled Christianity is one of the great needs of the day. There are too many Christians trying to do the work of God in the flesh. Jesus said, **the flesh profiteth nothing. (John 6:63)** We need a filling of the Holy Spirit that will result in power for service with souls being won and Christians growing in grace and knowledge. If the Holy Spirit is in charge, great changes will take place in the life and work of believers.

POWER AND THE SPIRIT FILLED LIFE

And be not drunk with wine, wherein is excess; but be filled with the Spirit. (Ephesians 5:18) Here is a double command. It is a negative command—**be not drunk** and it is a positive command—**be filled with the Spirit.** No one can do the work of God successfully without being filled with the Holy Spirit. Our Lord taught this truth just before His ascension.

> **And he said unto them, These are the words which I spake unto you, while I was yet with you, that all things must be fulfilled, which were written in the law of Moses, and in the prophets, and in the psalms, concerning me. Then opened he their understanding, that they might understand the scriptures, And said unto them, Thus it is written, and thus it behoved Christ to**

suffer, and to rise from the dead the third day: And that repentance and remission of sins should be preached in his name among all nations, beginning at Jerusalem. And ye are witnesses of these things. And, behold, I send the promise of my Father upon you: but tarry ye in the city of Jerusalem, until ye be endued with power from on high. (Luke 24:44-49)

What a lesson from our Saviour! Christ said, "I have finished what I came to do. I've suffered and died for the sins of the world and rose on the third day." Notice what He says next. **And ye are witnesses of these things** and in the very next verse, **I send the promise of my father upon you: but tarry ye in the city of Jerusalem, until ye be endued with power from on high.** He said you are to be my witnesses but you must stay here until the Holy Spirit comes upon you. Christ knew they couldn't do the work of God without first being filled with God!

The Apostle Paul said, **And be not drunk with wine, wherein is excess; but be filled with the Spirit. (Ephesians 5:18)** To be filled with the Holy Spirit does not mean that we have more of Him, but that He has more of us at His will. When we are saved we are indwelt by the Spirit of God. All Christians have the Holy Spirit living in them, ... **Now if any man have not the Spirit of Christ, he is none of his. (Romans 8:9)** Every child of God has all of the Holy Spirit that he will ever have. The issue is not that we get more of Him, but that he gets more of us. We must yield ourselves to Him allowing Him to take over and control us. God cannot fill that which has not first been emptied. We ask for fullness but we are already full of ourselves. The Holy Spirit cannot and will not work through a vessel that is unclean. To be filled with the Spirit is to be controlled by Him. Paul compares two kinds of influence, the influence of wine and the influence of the Spirit.

Paul is saying, just as alcohol will control your thoughts and actions, just as the drunkard gives himself over body, soul and spirit, all he is and all he has to alcohol, so give yourself over to the Holy Spirit. A Spirit filled Christian is controlled and dominated in thought, word and deed by the Holy Spirit. The result is power to serve God. Old fashioned, Holy Ghost power is the need of today and it has been promised to us. **But ye shall receive power, after that the Holy Ghost is come upon you: and ye shall be witnesses unto me both in Jerusalem, and in all Judaea, and in Samaria, and unto the uttermost part of the earth. (Acts 1:8)** The power of God in the Christian's life comes as a result of being Spirit filled.

PRAISE AND THE SPIRIT FILLED LIFE

Speaking to yourselves in psalms and hymns and spiritual songs, singing and making melody in your heart to the Lord; Giving thanks always for all things unto God and the Father in the name of our Lord Jesus Christ. (Ephesians 5:19-5:20) The Spirit-filled life is evidenced by an attitude of joy and worship. When we came to Christ and received Him as Saviour and His Holy Spirit took up residence in us, everything changed. When we allow the Spirit to control us we will have joy. The Spirit filled life is not only one of power, it is also a life of praise. The control of the Spirit is expressed in song and praise. Paul refers to six of the many results of being Spirit filled.

1) **Psalms.** This refers primarily to the Old Testament psalms put to music. However, the term was also used of other vocal music including solos and anthems. The word *"psalmos"* comes from the word *psao* which means *"to touch"* and it referred to the touching of stringed instruments. Thayer defines it as, *"striking the chords of a musical instrument."* Sorry Bob Jones, but the Bible is not against stringed instruments. Psalms are specifically songs accompanied by a stringed instrument.

2) **Hymns.** A hymn is specifically a song that tells forth how great someone or something is. In our context it refers to songs addressed directly to God which praise and exalt Him. This would refer to the wonderful old Hymns of the faith like *How Great Thou Art, Great Is Thy Faithfulness* and many others.

3) **Spiritual songs.** These are songs with doctrinal content and speak of the Christian experience. These are songs like *Amazing Grace, There Is Power In The Blood, Stand up for Jesus, The Old Account Was Settled*, etc.

4) **Singing and making melody in your heart to the Lord. Singing** refers to vocal praise, and **making melody with your heart** implies inaudible praise. Our singing is for God. First and foremost our music must be pleasing to the Lord. We hear a lot about preferences in Christian music. People are quick to tell us what kind of music they like. Whether you like it or whether I like it is not

the issue. The text says, **to the Lord.** The issue is whether or not God is pleased with it. The Contemporary Christian Music movement seems to have missed this point. I recently heard one of these modern musicians claim, *"My music is edifying to believers and I don't care who dislikes it."* He should care about whether or not God likes it. We are uplifted and edified by good Christian music, however, edification of the believer is not the main issue in Christian music. The real issue is, Does God approve of it? Keep this in mind. For music to be edifying to the saint, it must be acceptable to the Saviour.

5) **Giving thanks always for all things unto God and the Father in the name of our Lord Jesus Christ. (Ephesians 5:20)** The Spirit filled believer is a thankful believer. When you are Spirit filled you do not grumble about what you think you deserve and don't have, you praise God for all the good you do have that you don't deserve. **In every thing give thanks: for this is the will of God in Christ Jesus concerning you. (1 Thessalonians 5:18)** It is possible to be thankful in all things only when we recognize the Providence of God is at work in our lives.

6) **Submitting yourselves one to another in the fear of God. (Ephesians 5:21)** A Spirit filled Christian will be considerate of others. Notice the phrase, **one to another.** Considering others is not only important, but a must if we are to be fruitful as a Church. Paul warned the Philippians about this when he said, **Let nothing be done through strife or vainglory; but in lowliness of**

mind let each esteem other better than themselves. (Philippians 2:3) To be considerate of others is completely contrary to depraved human nature, but not to the new spiritual nature. The depraved and prideful man submits to no one. The Spirit filled man, because he is in submission to Christ, can submit to others. Mutual submission means readiness to renounce one's own will for the sake of others, to give priority to others.

The Biblical Wife
Ephesians 5:22-24

Paul moves on from the subject of the Spirit-filled life to expound on God's standard for the marriage relationship. The husband, the wife and the children all have divinely appointed places and responsibilities in the home. The husband is to lead, the wife is to follow and the children are to obey. First Paul deals with the responsibilities of the wife.

THE INSTRUCTION FOR SUBMISSION

Wives, submit yourselves unto your own husbands .... **(Ephesians 5:22a)** The biblical view of the husband/wife relationship is rejected by the Women's Liberation Movement, but it is God's way nevertheless. It must be understood that submission in no way suggests inferiority on the part of the one submitting. It is true that in Christ, **there is neither male nor female. (Galatians 3:28)** In relation to the equality of believers in the Lord there is no difference between the man and the woman. However, husbands and wives differ so far as their functions are concerned. God is a God of design and order. Submission has to do with order, not value. It is a matter of headship. **But I would have you know, that the head of every man is Christ; and the head of the woman is the man; and the head of Christ is God. (1 Corinthians 11:3)** Contrary to feminist propaganda, this verse does not imply that man is better or more valuable than woman. This verse tells us that God is the Head of Christ, Christ is the Head of man, and man is the head of the woman. When God says that the man is the head of the woman, He is not talking about value, competence, ability or advantage. God is talking about occupation and order within an organization. Every organization must have a head for it to be operated in an efficient and orderly manner. Those who work within the organization must willingly submit to the head. Otherwise there will be no unity and little or no success. God does have a divine order of authority in the Christian home.

Wives, submit yourselves unto your own husbands, as it is fit in the Lord. (Colossians 3:18) The word **fit** speaks of that which is proper and appropriate. The idea is that of meeting an obligation. This is God's plan for the home and we are obligated to obey. God has ordained the husband to be the authority and the wife is to follow him as he follows the Lord.

THE INCENTIVE FOR SUBMISSION

The wife is to submit **as unto the Lord. (Ephesians 5:22b)** Ladies, this brings Christ into the matter of submission to your husband. The idea here is to submit to your husband as an act of submission to the Lord. If a woman is submissive to Christ, submission to her husband will follow. When the Christian wife submits herself to Christ and lets Him be Lord of her life, she will have no difficulty submitting to her husband. John Philips said:

> "That perspective lifts this command to a higher, holier, and more heavenly plane. What woman in all the world who has met and fallen in love with Jesus would not willingly do anything for Him?"

Just as the wife has a duty to submit to Christ, she also has a duty to submit to her husband. It was God who tied these two together! Ladies, your husband is your earthy authority.

> **Likewise, ye wives, be in subjection to your own husbands; that, if any obey not the word, they also may without the word be won by the conversation of the wives; While they behold your chaste conversation coupled with fear. Whose adorning let it not be that outward adorning of plaiting the hair, and of wearing of gold, or of putting on of apparel; But let it be the hidden man of the heart, in that which is not corruptible, even the ornament of a meek and quiet spirit, which is in the sight of God of great price. For after this manner in the old time the holy women also, who trusted in God, adorned themselves, being in subjection unto their own husbands: Even as Sarah obeyed Abraham, calling him lord: whose daughters ye are, as long as ye do well, and are not afraid with any amazement. (1 Peter 3:1-6)**

There is an issue that must be addressed here. There is a big difference between the wife's voluntary submission and the husband's ungodly and cruel oppression. Kent Hughes said:

> ...the truths of this text have been perverted and abused by disordered and sinful men. God's holy Word in the hands of a religious fool can do immense harm. I have seen couch potatoes who order their wives and children around like the grand sultan of Morocco — adulterous misogynists with the domestic ethics of Jabba the Hut who cow their wives around with Bible verses about submission — insecure men whose wives do not dare go to the grocery store without permission, who even tell their wives how to dress. But the fact that evil, disordered

men have perverted God's Word is no reason to throw it out.

There are those who foolishly teach that a wife is to submit to every whim and quirk of her husband without question. The wife is to never do anything that is sinful. Just like Christ would never command His Church to do wrong, the husband is not to require of his wife to do that which would displease the Lord. The **as unto the Lord** command does not mean that their husband is their god, but rather that the wife's submission to her husband is a duty which she owes to the Lord.

THE ILLUSTRATION OF SUBMISSION

For the husband is the head of the wife, even as Christ is the head of the church: and he is the saviour of the body. Therefore as the church is subject unto Christ, so let the wives be to their own husbands in every thing. (Ephesians 5:23-24) Paul continues to press the issue. He wants this to be understood. In the New Testament Church, there is a definite head, the Lord Jesus Christ. And in the home there is a definite head, the husband. The husband is the head of the wife, even as Christ is the head of the Church. This does not mean the man is a bully and a dictator. He is not a slave driver, but He is God's authoritative leader over his home. There will be issues that arise when the man of the house must stand and say this is how it is. There is no compromise. However, the man who does not consult his wife and locks her out of everything is indeed a poor leader. In fact, he is no leader at all.

The Biblical Husband
Ephesians 5:25-33

Paul was not a one sided preacher. After dealing with the wife's responsibility to submit to her husband he commands the husband to love his wife as Christ loved the Church. Leadership carries with it great responsibility.

THE EXHORTATION

Husbands, love your wives.... (Ephesians 5:25a) To the people of Paul's day it was not surprising that Paul commanded the women to submit to their husbands. The women of that day were basically looked at as servants of their husbands. They had little or no rights, but lots of responsibility. Marriage was one-sided in that day—all for the husband and very little for the wife. It was a man's world. However, Christianity changed all of that. Under inspiration of the Holy Spirit, Paul did not encourage husbands to be a dictator, commanding and bossing their wives around, but to love their wives. The Biblical command to **love your wives** ran against the grain of popular opinion and established love as the husband's supreme marital duty.

THE EXAMPLE

The example is clear, we are to love our wives **even as Christ also loved the church, and gave himself for it. (Ephesians 5:25b)** Having exhorted husbands to love their wives, Paul speaks of the quality of love that God requires. By using the word *"agape,"* Paul took the marital relationship to a new and higher level. The Greeks had four different words that described the different kinds of love.

1) **Sexual Love** from the word *"eros."* This word refers to romantic or sexual love and is not used in the Bible.

2) **Family Love** from the word *"storge."* This is a family love—the kind of love there is between a parent and child, or between family members in general. This word is not used in the New Testament.

3) **Friendship Love** from the word *"phileo."* This is a love of a friendship and affection—brotherly love. It is the love of close friendship. It is the highest love of which man, without God's help, is capable of.

4) **Spiritual Love** from the word *"agape."* This is a sacrificial love, a love that gives itself for the person loved. It is the kind of love that demands something of us and nothing of the one loved.

It is *"agape"* love with which Paul commands husbands to love their wives. Paul uses the supreme example of Christ's redeeming love. We are to love our wives **even as Christ also loved the church, and gave himself for it. (Ephesians 5:25b)** Agape love is a sacrificing love that gives and asks for nothing in return. It is the kind of love that God has for sinners (John 3:16). The evidence of His unwavering love is the sacrifice of His Son for the sin of a lost world.

> **But God commendeth his love toward us, in that, while we were yet sinners, Christ died for us. (Romans 5:8)**

God did not say *"if you meet my standard, I will give My Son for you."* Jesus never required anything of us before He would die for our sin. He lovingly, voluntarily and sacrificially laid His life down for us. This is the kind of love that knows no boundaries. It is sacrificial to the end. It is not seeking, it is giving. It is a love that is never selfish, self-serving, and self-seeking. The husband who loves his wife for what she can give him loves as the world loves, not as Christ loves. Husbands must study the life of Christ to understand how to love their wives.

THE EFFECT

That he might sanctify and cleanse it with the washing of water by the word. (Ephesians 5:26) The love of God has a powerful effect upon the Church. For husbands to love their wives as Christ loves His bride is to love them with a purifying love. Divine love does not simply condemn wrong in those loved, but seeks to cleanse them from it. **Come now, and let us reason together, saith the LORD: though your sins be as scarlet, they shall be as white as snow; though they be red like crimson, they shall be as wool. (Isaiah 1:18)** The love of Christ has a continual cleansing effect upon the saved. **If we confess our sins, he is faithful and just to forgive us our sins, and to cleanse us from all unrighteousness. (1 John 1:9)** The idea here is that this kind of love seeks only the best for the one it loves. When a husband has this kind of love for his wife, he will seek to help her become and stay pure, helping and encouraging her to walk with Christ.

THE ENDEAVOR

That he might present it to himself a glorious church, not having spot, or wrinkle, or any such thing; but that it should be holy and without blemish. (Ephesians 5:27) Agape love improves and makes one better. Paul says **not having spot, or wrinkle, or any such thing.** Christ's bride will not be totally without sin until she has passed through the Judgment Seat Of Christ. However, Christ is regularly conforming us to His image, purifying us as we submit to him. The idea is that our wives may not be perfect, but they should be advancing as a result of the husbands love.

THE EXTENT

So ought men to love their wives as their own bodies. He that loveth his wife loveth himself. For no man ever yet hated his own flesh; but nourisheth and cherisheth it, even as the Lord the church: For we are members of his body, of his flesh, and of his bones. For this cause shall a man leave his father and mother, and shall be joined unto his wife, and they two shall be one flesh. (Ephesians 5:28-31) Paul uses another scriptural illustration to teach us the extent of the husband's love for his wife. Paul commands that husbands are to love their wives as **their own bodies.** In verse 31, Paul says that the husband and wife **shall be one flesh.** The idea is that a husband who views his wife as being one with him can love her in a sacrificial and edifying way because he sees her as part of himself and **no man ever yet hated his own flesh; but nourisheth and cherisheth it.** Just as a husband cares for himself he is to care for his wife. This is exactly what our Lord is doing for His bride.

THE ECHO

This is a great mystery: but I speak concerning Christ and the church. Nevertheless let every one of you in particular so love his wife even as himself; and the wife see that she reverence her husband. (Ephesians 5:32-33) Paul simply reiterates what he has already said concerning the husband's and wife's responsibility to one another. The husband is to **love his wife** and the wife to **reverence** her husband.

Obedience In The Home
Ephesians 6:1-4

After clearly laying out the responsibilities of Husbands and wives, Paul deals with the children.

THE PRINCIPLE OF OBEDIENCE

Children, obey your parents in the Lord.... (Ephesians 6:1a) This is a command that has sounded out through the ages and is needed more in our day than ever before. Never in history have children been so disobedient and disrespectful to parents as in this present day. Noah Webster defines **obey** as *"to comply with the commands, orders or instructions of a superior, or with the requirements of law, moral, political or municipal; to do that which is commanded or required, or to forbear doing that which is prohibited."* According to James Strong the word **obey** means *"to hear under (as a subordinate), i.e. to listen attentively; by implication to heed or conform to a command or authority."* This is an interesting word. It was used in Bible times of a doorkeeper. He first heard the knock, then acted upon what he heard by opening the door. The meaning here is that the child is to listen, then act in accordance to what he hears. This word combines both the responsibilities of hearing and doing. Children are to listen to their parents with earnest attention and respond positively to what is heard. Children are to obediently and humbly put themselves under the words and authority of their parents. Understand that delayed obedience is disobedience and incomplete obedience is disobedience. There is no middle ground. Obedience is not an option. Being **disobedient to parents, (Romans 1:30)** is a characteristic of the heathen. Paul also states that children being **disobedient to parents, (2 Timothy 3:2)** is a sign of the apostasy that will prevail in the last days. When you, as a young person disobey your parents, you are acting like a heathen apostate. You say, "Preacher, that's pretty strong talk." It may be, but that is what God thinks about disobedience. The Bible says, **My son, hear the instruction of thy father, and forsake not the law of thy mother. (Proverbs 1:8)** God told Saul, **To obey is better than sacrifice. (1 Samuel 15:22)** Obedience is a serious matter to God.

THE PURPOSE OF OBEDIENCE

Why all the fuss over obedience? Why does God make such a big deal out of obeying mom and dad? Paul answers that in the latter part of verse one. Children are to obey their parents **for this is right. (Ephesians 6:1b)** Enough of the questions and debates. Young people listen up. When you are told by your parents to do something or not to do something, Do not ask why? Do not come back and try to debate the issue. Once you do that, you have failed in obedience. Your parents know when your room needs to be cleaned. They know what music you should be listening to. They know what you shouldn't be watching on TV. When your parents give the instruction, simply obey them **for this is right.**

THE PERFORMANCE OF OBEDIENCE

Honour thy father and mother.... (Ephesians 6:2a) Paul goes back and quotes the fifth commandment. **Honour thy father and thy mother.... (Exodus 20:12)** The word **honour** means *"to hold worthy; to value; to respect."* The noun speaks of a *"place of honor or rank."* Respect and honor for parents is of such grave importance to God that Moses commanded:

> **And he that smiteth his father, or his mother, shall be surely put to death. (Exodus 21:15)**

> **And he that curseth his father, or his mother, shall surely be put to death. (Exodus 21:17)**

> **For every one that curseth his father or his mother shall be surely put to death: he hath cursed his father or his mother; his blood shall be upon him. (Leviticus 20:9)**

Honor and obedience are very different. Obedience has to do with action, honor has to do with attitude. Not only are young people to obey their parents, they are to think right and have a good attitude about it. You may not always understand your parent's decisions and directions, but you are to honor and respect them.

THE PROMISE OF OBEDIENCE

Honour thy father and mother; (which is the first commandment with promise;) That it may be well with thee, and thou mayest live long on the earth. (Ephesians 6:2-3) There are two wonderful promises attached to the command of obedience.

First, **That it may be well with thee.** The word **well** means *"good and prosperous"* and speaks of the quality of life. It's not hard to notice that it is not well with a lot of young people today. Our present generation of pleasure seeking young people are the most down-hearted, depressed and despondent in history. Pleasure does not produce happiness. The statistics are horrifying. The American Academy of Child and Adolescent Psychiatry says, "Statistics show that suicide is the third leading cause of death among those 15 to 25 years of age, and it is the sixth leading cause of death among those 5 to 14 years of age. It is estimated that 500,000 teenagers try to kill themselves every year, and about 5,000 succeed." In addition, there are over 3 million teenage alcoholics and several million more who drink. There are millions of others who are slaves to drugs, illicit sex and other wickedness. It is not well with the world's young people and in most cases it started with disobedience to parents. I recently asked a young man, a 20 year old preparing for the ministry, "How is everything going?" He answered, "Life is good!" What a refreshing contrast to the sad answer that most teens would give to that question.

Second, that **thou mayest live long on the earth.** The first promise has to do with quality of life while the second has to do with quantity of life. This is the promise of a long life for those who obey and honor their parents. Young people need to take this to heart. Samson and Absalom are two Scriptural examples of boys who did not follow this commandment, and their lives were cut short. Samson fell far short of God's desire for his life and died when he was a young man. Absalom rebelled against his father David, and he was killed when he was a young man.

Children who have no respect for their Christian parents, who are breaking their hearts by the things they do, the places they go, the company they run with, will not live to a ripe old age. Honoring your parents promises life and blessings on the earth. However, if you are deliberately disobeying godly parents, rest assured that you will reap what you sow.

THE PREVENTION OF OBEDIENCE

And, ye fathers, provoke not your children to wrath.... (Ephesians 6:4a) The responsibility is not one-sided. Parents have a great responsibility and role to play in their children's obedience. Paul is basically instructing parents to consider their children as they discipline and carry out their responsibilities as parents. This was a radical concept in the first-century world where the father had absolute authority. Fathers, thc idca that Paul is putting across here is that even with God-given authority behind us we do not have the right to be unfair. The word **provoke** means to *"arouse to wrath or anger, to provoke to the point of utter exasperation and resentment."* There are several ways that parents provoke their children to wrath.

A Prideful Parent

Many parents have a *"because I said so"* mentality in raising their kids. That may work for a little while, but as your kids grow up into teenagers and young adults it is only natural that they grow in their wisdom and understanding. This is why we are commanded to train our children. **Train up a child in the way he should go: and when he is old, he will not depart from it. (Proverbs 22:6)** The word train is an interesting one. It means to teach and discipline, but it comes from a word that carries the idea of, "to influence the taste." It was originally used of a mother dipping her finger in honey and rubbing on a new born baby's gums. The honey would affect the baby's taste and start him to nursing. Parents train and teach their children by influencing their taste—teaching them what pleases and displeases God. As the child grows into a teenager and young adult, parents must gradually give them the responsibility of following the principle that we have helped them to establish in their lives.

A Pitiless Parent

A parent who is harsh and hard in their rules and expectations will produce an angry child. I have seen many kids driven away from God because of unreasonable and unrealistic demands of parents. This is also a big problem with leadership. I have seen folks as soon as they get a little authority, they start making a list of rules. A lot of people look at leadership as an opportunity to publicize, promote, and propagate their ideas instead of an opportunity to lead. A religion of rules and regulations is exactly what has hurt Fundamentalism over the years. We have standards and rules and we need them—I am for standards. But standards and rules without grace is Phariseism. The Bible says, **Mercy and truth preserve the king: and his throne is upholden by mercy. (Proverbs 20:28)** Notice that it is **mercy and truth** that preserve the King, not just truth. If you want your family to last and if you want to have a preserving effect on your kids you had better rule with mercy. Notice that the king's **throne is upholden by mercy.** The throne speaks of the king's authority. We must have a combination of mercy and truth that preserves our rule.

It is OK to restrict your child's activities. There are certain places that they shouldn't be allowed to go. By the same token there are places that they can go. There is music that shouldn't be allowed, but there is also some good music out there. There are some awful movies that shouldn't be allowed under any circumstances. However, there are a lot of good movies that will not hurt your children. In fact it will help them. Someone said, I'm not going to let my children sit around a TV and laugh and giggle. Well aren't you a spiritual giant? What alternative are you offering them? The Bible says, **A merry heart doeth good like a medicine: but a broken spirit drieth the bones. (Proverbs 17:22)**

Have you ever noticed how some young people are so miserable? They walk around looking like they were weaned on pickle juice. They have never learned to laugh. What a pity! Let them watch a movie and laugh a little. It is good for them. Let them play a silly board game—it's alright to have fun. Balance is not a bad word. Making unreasonable demands of your children will hurt them just as much as having no restrictions at all. Overbearing and out of balance rules are going to harden your kids against the things of God to the point that all they are going to look forward to is turning 18 and getting out from under your rule. At that point you will forever lose your influence in their life. An unbalanced approach to child training has driven more young people out of the service of God than into it. Have a balance. Don't over react! You don't need a cannon to kill a mosquito.

A Prejudice Parent

A parent who is one-sided and shows favoritism to another child is in for serious trouble. We have to be careful here. **I charge thee before God, and the Lord Jesus Christ, and the elect angels, that thou observe these things without preferring one before another, doing nothing by partiality. (1 Timothy 5:21)** Partiality is a big problem and it always has been. Isaac was partial to Esau and favored him over Jacob. Rebekah preferred Jacob over Esau. What serious problems were produced because of their partiality and it will cause serious problems in your life as well.

A Phony Parent

Young people can spot a hypocrite a mile off. If you are not living what you are preaching you will greatly hinder your kids. I've seen parents who smoke try to teach their kids that is wrong to use tobacco. Parents who use foul language try to teach their kids that is wrong to cuss. Parents who cheat on their taxes and brag about it try to teach their children that it is wrong to cheat on their school work. Solomon said, **An hypocrite with his mouth destroyeth his neighbour. (Proverbs 11:9)** If you say one thing with your lips and do another with your life you will provoke your children to wrath.

THE PROPAGATION OF OBEDIENCE

Parents are admonished to **bring them up in the nurture and admonition of the Lord. (Ephesians 6:4)** Rather than push and provoke them, we are to **bring them up.** The phrase translated **bring them up** is the same word translated **nourisheth** in Ephesians 5:29. It means *"to feed; to clothe; to nurture; to look after..."* The idea is that of a shepherd caring for his sheep. You don't drive sheep, you lead them by bringing them along. The word **nurture** carries with it the idea of correcting or chastening. The word **admonition** means to rebuke or correct with words. The responsibility for child rearing is a great one. We must be diligent about accomplishing it in a way that will produce young people who will bring glory to God.

Masters And Servants
Ephesians 6:5-9

We come to the relationship between slaves and masters. The application would be to the employee/employer.

THE PRINCIPLE OF SUBMISSION

Servants, be obedient to them that are your masters according to the flesh ... (Ephesians 6:5a) In all of the relationships mentioned, we see that submission is crucial. Wives are to submit to their husbands (5:22). Children are to obey their parents (6:1). Servants are to obey their masters. The word **obedient** comes from the Greek *"hypakouo"* and means *"to hear under as a subordinate, to heed or conform to a command."* The word **masters** comes from *"kyrios"* and means *"one who in authority."* Christians are to obey their employers. We are to follow their instructions and put in a full day's work for a full day's pay. The boss is there to tell the employee what to do, not the other way around.

THE PERFORMANCE OF SUBMISSION

... with fear and trembling, in singleness of your heart, as unto Christ; Not with eyeservice, as menpleasers; but as the servants of Christ, doing the will of God from the heart; With good will doing service, as to the Lord, and not to men: (Ephesians 6:5b-7) Now Paul says that the Christian is to serve his employer ... **as unto Christ ... doing service, as to the Lord.** The employee is to consider his service as being rendered directly to the Lord. Anyone who takes this passage seriously will have a good work ethic.

Servants are to serve **with fear and trembling.** The Greek word for **fear** is *"phobos"* and means fear, alarm, fright, terror. Webster defines fear as, *"an unpleasant often strong* *emotion caused by an awareness of danger."* The word for **trembling** is *"tromos,"* from which we get our English word tremor. It means to means *"to shake or quake with fear."* The idea it that the servant obeys and respects his master with an awareness that he is going to answer to God.

Such service is to be carried out ... **in singleness of your heart.** The word **singleness** comes from the Greek *"haplotes"* and means *"sincerity, without hypocrisy, pretense or self-seeking."* What God is requiring here whole-hearted submission and serve to our employers.

Not with eyeservice, as menpleasers... The idea here that we don't just work because the boss is watching. We don't serve to be seen of men, we serve because it is the **will of God** and we know He is watching.

THE PAYMENT FOR SUBMISSION

Knowing that whatsoever good thing any man doeth, the same shall he receive of the Lord, whether he be bond or free. (Ephesians 6:8) Obedience certainly has its rewards and so does disobedience. This is the principle of sowing and reaping. In the day of judgment we will receive from the Lord the reward for our obedience.

And, ye masters, do the same things unto them, forbearing threatening: knowing that your Master also is in heaven; neither is there respect of persons with him. (Ephesians 6:9) Employers also have an obligation to see to that they treat their employees right. They too, will answer to God for their action and **there respect of persons with him**. At the judgment, God will deal with both boss and worker the same way. The boss man may have a superior position in the workplace, but in Heaven the only superior position is held by God and He will be the Righteous Judge.

Stand Up For Jesus
Ephesians 6:10-20

No one who is serious about pleasing God and doing His will can go through life without meeting opposition. The god of this world and the powers of darkness are enemies of God and His people. There are several things we learn from this passage of Scripture.

OUR EFFICIENCY

Finally, my brethren, be strong in the Lord, and in the power of his might. (Ephesians 6:10) We see from the start that our victory is dependent upon our relationship with Christ. It is because of Christ's work on the cross that we can have victory over Satan. The believer's efficiency for the battle is **in the Lord.** Any victory we have is a result of His finished work on Calvary's cross. We have no strength in ourselves. All our strength and victory is in Christ. The Bible declares that through His work on the cross, Christ **spoiled principalities and powers and made a show of them openly, triumphing over them in it. (Colossians 2:15)**

A Conquered Enemy

Our victory is **in the Lord, and in the power of his might. (Ephesians 6:10b)** Satan is a defeated foe when it comes to the Christian. Christ broke Satan's power and authority over helpless sinners. His death redeemed sinners while at the same time passing judgment upon Satan and his demons. The Lord Jesus Christ has conquered the enemy. He **spoiled principalities and powers. (Colossians 2:15a)** The word **spoiled** carries the idea of *"putting off or stripping away."* It is used here of Christ stripping Satan of authority. The devil is a defeated foe with no authority over the believer.

A Celebrated Event

Jesus **... made a shew of them openly, triumphing over them in it. (Colossians 2:15b)** The metaphor used here in Colossians 2:15 is that of a triumphant King returning home after battle, leading his captives and displaying the spoils of war in a celebration parade. Christ's sacrifice on the cross disarmed Satan and his wicked hosts, stripping them of their powers. Not only did Jesus conquer Satan, but He celebrated the victory. The phrase, **He made a shew of them openly** speaks of a victory celebration after the battle. The word **shew** means to *"exhibit, display, publish, or proclaim."* It is the same word used of Mary when Joseph did not **make her a publick example. (Matthew 1:19)** The word **triumphing** speaks of *"an open parade."* Once the battle was over and won, the triumphant emperor would return home and victoriously parade the prisoners that he had captured during his military conquest.

A Continuing Effect

The finished work of Christ in the shedding of His Blood has continuing results. Satan has no chance of ever winning. He is a defeated enemy. In the book of Revelation we see that God's people **overcame him by the blood of the Lamb... (Revelation 12:11)** The same Blood that saves, secures, and sustains also strengthens. The Blood will never lose its power. It is because of the finished work of Christ that the Christian soldier can overcome and walk in victory. Christians are Victors, not Victims. **For whatsoever is born of God overcometh the world: and this is the victory that**

overcometh the world, even our faith. (1 John 5:4) The Christian's victory over Satan is guaranteed by the shed Blood of Christ and His atoning work at Calvary. He will never recover from that death blow.

OUR ENERGY

We are to be strong in the Lord and **in the power of his might. (Ephesians 6:10)** We must understand that we do not battle in our strength and power. **Not by might, nor by power, but by my spirit, saith the LORD of hosts. (Zechariah 4:6)** We must rely upon a stronger and more powerful resource. **For the weapons of our warfare are not carnal, but mighty through God to the pulling down of strong holds. (2 Corinthians 10:4)** The Holy Spirit is the fulfilled promise of Jesus Christ to His own and is the Christian's source of supernatural power. Jesus commissioned His people to reach the world with the gospel message. It is the greatest and most important duty that was ever laid upon human hearts and entrusted to human hands. **But ye shall receive power, after that the Holy Ghost is come upon you: and ye shall be witnesses unto me both in Jerusalem, and in all Judaea, and in Samaria, and unto the uttermost part of the earth. (Acts 1:8)** There must be supernatural power to perform this task. Jesus provides that power through the filling of the Holy Spirit.

OUR ENEMY

For we wrestle not against flesh and blood, but against principalities, against powers, against the rulers of the darkness of this world, against spiritual wickedness in high places. (Ephesians 6:12) We face a whole army of demonic forces. They are listed as **principalities ... powers**

... rulers of the darkness ... spiritual wickedness in high places. Satan has plenty of help in combating God's people.

The word **wrestle** comes from the Greek *"pale"* and speaks of hand-to-hand combat. This is not long distance battle. This is personal, up-close, in-your-face warfare. In Paul's day as in our own, wrestling was characterized by trickery and deception. We face an enemy who is the master of deceit. That is why we are commanded to **Put on the whole armour of God, that ye may be able to stand against the wiles of the devil. (Ephesians 6:11)** The word **wiles** comes from *"methodeias."* It is the word from which we get *"method."* It is a word that is connected with evil doing and carries the idea of being *"cunning and crafty."* Paul warned the Corinthians **... Satan himself is transformed into an angel of light. (2 Corinthians 11:14)** Satan has methods that he uses in his attempt to defeat and destroy God's people. He is a ruthless enemy with a host of powerful forces who will stop at nothing in hopes of defeating Christians.

OUR EQUIPMENT

Wherefore take unto you the whole armour of God, that ye may be able to withstand in the evil day, and having done all, to stand. (Ephesians 6:13) The emphasis is on the **whole armour**. The word for **whole armour** is *"panoplia"* and emphasizes *"every piece of armour."* The idea is that every single piece of armour is to be used.

Our Sash

Stand therefore, having your loins girt about with truth. (Ephesians 6:14) This piece of armour is in reference to the belt which the Roman soldier wore around his waist. It's purpose was to hold and keep the other pieces of his armor in place. The soldier's armor must remain intact at all times. Without this belt the other parts of his armor would move around and get out of place becoming a hindrance rather than a help in battle. The Christian soldier must be **girt about with truth.** The belt of truth is what holds everything in place. Unfortunately, in our day many see truth as relative rather than absolute.

In His high priestly prayer on the behalf of all believers, Jesus asked the **Father to Sanctify them through thy truth: thy word is truth. (John 17:17)** A Christian soldier will not survive apart from the Word of God. The Apostle Paul said under inspiration of the Holy Spirit, **So then faith cometh by hearing, and hearing by the word of God. (Romans 10:17)** Faith is built by the Word of God. Everything we need for this war is found in the Word of God. **All scripture is given by inspiration of God, and is profitable for doctrine, for reproof, for correction, for instruction in righteousness: That the man of God may be perfect, thoroughly furnished unto all good works. (2 Timothy 3:16-17)** It is through the Word of God that the believer is strengthened to continue his walk with God. The Word of God makes the difference between spiritual survival and failure. **Unless thy law had been my delights, I should then have perished in mine affliction. (Psalm 119:92)** It is the Word of God that instructs us on how to keep it together.

Our Salvation

The next piece of armour has to do with our salvation and righteousness. Paul adds, **and having on the breastplate of righteousness. (Ephesians 6:14)** The breastplate covered the body, protecting the heart and other vital organs from injury. The Christian's breastplate is righteousness. He must be righteous in God's eyes as well as man's. This is both positional and practical.

First, **_Positional Righteousness_**. At the moment of salvation we are declared righteous by God. We are made righteous in Christ. **But to him that worketh not, but believeth on him that justifieth the ungodly, his faith is counted for righteousness. (Romans 4:5)** The words **count, impute,** and **reckon** all come from the same word. This is a word that comes from the business world and carries the idea of *"crediting an account."* It would be like going to the bank and depositing $10,000. The bank applies that money to your account. We come to Christ as bankrupt sinners. We are broke and have no righteousness of our own, but when we, by faith trust in Christ, God takes out the book and credits Christ's righteousness to our account. **For he hath made him to be sin for us, who knew no sin; that we might be made the righteousness of God in him. (2 Corinthians 5:21)**

Second, **_Practical Righteousness_**. God has made wonderful provision whereby we can maintain our fellowship with Him through the blood of our Lord Jesus Christ. **If we confess our sins, he is faithful and just to forgive us our sins, and to cleanse us from all unrighteousness. (1 John 1:9)** The Christian soldier must be cleansed from **all unrighteousness.** The word **confess** comes from the compound word *"homologeo."* Made up of *"homos"* meaning *"the same,"* and *"lego"* meaning *"to say."* It means say the same thing. It carries the idea of *"agreeing with another."* Confession is to acknowledge and say the same thing about sin that God says. David in his confession said, **Against thee, thee only, have I sinned, and done this evil in thy sight ... (Psalm 51:4)** It might also be noted that the word **confess** is in the present tense, emphasizing the need for continuous confessing. To succeed in battle all sin must be confessed and forgiven. A pure heart and a clean life are essential to the Christian soldier's defense against the assaults of evil.

Our Shoes

Your feet shod with the preparation of the gospel of peace. (Ephesians 6:15) Having our feet shod with the proper shoes speaks of a sure footing. The Roman soldier wore shoes that were studded and cleated to ensure good footing. The word **preparation** carries the idea of being prepared and ready. The soldier properly shod is ready to engage in battle on a moment's notice. Properly shod, he is able to stand in slippery places, to endure long hard marches, and to walk over objects that otherwise would wound and damage his feet.

Notice also that these aren't ordinary shoes but shoes of **peace.** The **gospel of peace** always prepares the believer to go into battle with the right spirit. This speaks of the peace that we have in Christ, the peace secured for by His death on the cross. **And, having made peace through the blood of his cross, by him to reconcile all things unto himself. (Colossians 1:20)** Because we are Saved, Sustained, Secured and Supported in Christ, we can engage in spiritual warfare with peace in our heart and life. **The LORD will give strength unto his people; the LORD will bless his people with peace. (Psalm 29:11)**

Our Shield

The shield of faith. (Ephesians 6:16) The Roman soldier's shield was made of wood, about four feet long and two feet wide and was covered with leather. It was carried on the forearm, and moved from side to side to break the force of arrows and other weapons. Notice the statement, ... **wherewith ye shall be able to quench all the fiery darts of the wicked."** The enemy would dip tips of their arrows in pitch and set them on fire before releasing them from their bows. Soldiers would soak their shields in water before the battle. This enabled them not only to stop the enemy's arrow's but also to quench the fire.

The Christian soldier's shield is faith. God demands faith and the Bible declares that, **without faith it is impossible to please him. (Hebrews 11:6)** Faith is taking God at His Word. The soldier operates with faith in his commanding officer. Our Lord has won the victory for us, and because of His finished work on Calvary the Devil is already defeated. By faith we are able to overcome. **For whatsoever is born of God overcometh the world: and this is the victory that overcometh the world, even our faith. (1 John 5:4)**

Our Security

And take the helmet of salvation. (Ephesians 6:17) The soldier's head stood above the shield, in plain view of the enemy and open to attack. The helmet served as protection for the soldier's head. The Bible has much to say about the importance of the mind (Philippians 2:5, Romans 12:2, 1 Peter 1:13).

The Christian soldier must protect his mind from Satanic attacks. The head is one of the most vulnerable parts of our body. Satan so often attacks through the mind with evil thoughts, doubts, fears, and discouragement. The shield did not make the soldier's defense complete. The same is true of the Christian soldier's shield of faith. Because we who practice faith so often fail, God adds further protection. Notice that this is no ordinary helmet, but the **helmet of salvation.** So often Christian soldiers become discouraged and lower their shield of faith opening themselves up to defeat and destruction. Faith is limited because of our weakness. However, that which our faith cannot do, God does for us. Salvation is God's gift to us because of His wonderful grace. What faith lacks, God's grace supplies.

Our Sword

Now we are to take up the **sword of the Spirit, which is the word of God. (Ephesians 6:17b)** The Sword is the Word of God. This is the only weapon of offense mentioned by Paul in the Christian warrior's equipment. The Sword of the Spirit is the Bible, the verbally inspired, infallible, inerrant, preserved and perfect Word of God. When our Lord was led up into the wilderness to be tempted He met the Devil's assault with the Word of God. Jesus met every attack with, **It is written ... (Matthew 4:4,6,7,10)** Through the ages the Bible has been the Sword by which Christian soldiers have driven back the enemies of Christ. No enemy sword or weapon is of equal value to the sword which God as forged for His soldiers. No wonder Satan and his wicked men have attempted so desperately to destroy the Bible.

Our Supplication

Praying always with all prayer and supplication in the Spirit. (Ephesians 6:18) The attitude of the Christian soldier's mind is to be one of continual prayer. Prayer moves the hand and heart of God. Notice that Paul said, **Praying always.** Without continual prayer the soldier will be defeated and fail in his duty to war a good warfare. Sam P.

Jones said, *"No man was ever conquered on his knees in prayer to God."* The Bible says, **Men ought always to pray, and not to faint. (Luke 18:1)** and **Pray without ceasing. (1 Thessalonians 5:17)** Continual prayer is prevailing prayer. Prayer must be persistent.

Paul further instructs, ...**watching thereunto with all perseverance and supplication for all saints. (Ephesians 6:18b)** The word **watching** comes from *"agrypneo"* and means *"sleepless."* We must sometimes miss out on sleep and relaxation in order to spend time with God. James reminds us that, **The effectual fervent prayer of a righteous man availeth much. (James 5:16)** Notice, the Bible instructs the soldier to pray with **all perseverance.** The word perseverance means *"to be earnest towards or on every occasion."* The Christian soldier will never face a battle that can't be overcome by prayer. Prayer is the Christian's spiritual strategy. We must not forget that ...**we wrestle not against flesh and blood, but against principalities, against powers, against the rulers of the darkness of this world, against spiritual wickedness in high places.** Such a battle would be suicide for us if we attempted to fight the enemy in the flesh. God has provided us with the armor and supplies to fight with. At the end of the list of armor which God has provided is prayer! Someone has well said, "Satan trembles when he sees even the weakest Christian on his knees." As Christian soldiers, we must persist in prayer. The old timers would say *"we must pray through."* They were speaking of praying until the answer came. The Christian stands best on his knees.

Made in the USA
Columbia, SC
25 June 2025

59863359R00100